Chapter 1	WTO Explained
Chapter 2	Basis of Trade
Chapter 3	Open Trade
Chapter 4	Development of GATT
Chapter 5	Uruguay Round
Chapter 6	WTO Agreements
Chapter 7	Reducing Tariffs
Chapter 8	Reforms in Agriculture
Chapter 9	Technical Barriers to Trade & Textiles
Chapter 10	GATS
Chapter 11	Intellectual Property
Chapter 12	Anti Dumping and SCM
Chapter 13	Trade policy review mechanism
Chapter 14	Regional trade agreements

Chapter 1

WTO Explained:-

There are a number of ways of looking at the WTO. It's an organization for liberalizing trade. It's a forum for governments to negotiate trade agreements. It's a place for them to settle trade disputes. It operates a system of trade rules. (But it's not Superman, just in case anyone thought it could solve — or cause — all the world's problems!)

Above all, it's a negotiating forum …
Essentially, the WTO is a place where member governments go, to try to sort out the trade problems they face with each other. The first step is to talk. The WTO was born out of negotiations, and everything the WTO does is the result of negotiations. The bulk of the WTO's current work comes from the 1986-94 negotiations called the Uruguay Round and earlier negotiations under the General Agreement on Tariffs and Trade (GATT). The WTO is currently the host to new negotiations, under the "Doha Development Agenda" launched in 2001.

Where countries have faced trade barriers and wanted them lowered, the negotiations have helped to liberalize trade. But the WTO is not just about liberalizing trade, and in some circumstances its rules support maintaining trade barriers — for example to protect consumers or prevent the spread of disease.

It's a set of rules … At its heart are the WTO agreements, negotiated and signed by the bulk of the world's trading nations. These documents provide the legal ground-rules for international commerce. They are essentially contracts, binding governments to keep their trade policies within agreed limits. Although negotiated and signed by governments, the goal is to help producers of goods and services, exporters, and importers conduct their business, while allowing governments to meet social and environmental objectives.

The system's overriding purpose is to help trade flow as freely as possible — so long as there are no undesirable side-effects — because this is important for economic development and well-being. That partly means removing obstacles. It also means ensuring that individuals, companies and governments know what the trade rules are around the world, and giving them the confidence that there will be no sudden changes of policy. In other words, the rules have to be "transparent" and predictable.

And it helps to settle disputes … This is a third important side to the WTO's work. Trade relations often involve conflicting interests. Agreements, including those painstakingly negotiated in the WTO system, often need interpreting. The most harmonious way to settle these differences is through some neutral procedure based on an agreed legal foundation. That is the purpose behind the dispute settlement process written into the WTO agreements.

Born in 1995, but not so young

The WTO began life on 1 January 1995, but its trading system is half a century older. Since 1948, the General Agreement on Tariffs and Trade (GATT) had provided the rules for the system. (The second WTO ministerial meeting, held in Geneva in May 1998, included a celebration of the 50th anniversary of the system.)

It did not take long for the General Agreement to

give birth to an unofficial, *de facto* international organization, also known informally as GATT. Over the years GATT evolved through several rounds of negotiations.

The last and largest GATT round, was the Uruguay Round which lasted from 1986 to 1994 and led to the WTO's creation. Whereas GATT had mainly dealt with trade in goods, the WTO and its agreements now cover trade in services, and in traded inventions, creations and designs (intellectual property).

Chapter 2

Basis of Trade

1. Most-favoured-nation (MFN): treating other people equally Under the WTO agreements, countries cannot normally discriminate between their trading partners. Grant someone a special favour (such as a lower customs duty rate for one of their products) and you have to do the same for all other WTO members.

This principle is known as most-favoured-nation (MFN) treatment (_see box_). It is so important that it is the first article of the General Agreement on Tariffs and Trade (GATT), which governs trade in goods. MFN is also a priority in the General Agreement on Trade in Services (GATS) (Article 2) and the Agreement on Trade-Related Aspects of Intellectual Property Rights (TRIPS) (Article 4), although in each agreement the principle is handled slightly differently. Together, those three agreements cover all three main areas of trade handled by the WTO.

Some exceptions are allowed. For example, countries can set up a free trade agreement that applies only to goods traded within the group — discriminating against goods from outside. Or they can give developing countries special access to their markets. Or a country can raise barriers against products that are considered to be traded unfairly from specific countries. And in services, countries are allowed, in limited circumstances, to discriminate. But the agreements only permit these exceptions under strict conditions. In general, MFN means that every time a country lowers a trade barrier or opens up a market, it has to do so for the same goods or services from all its trading partners — whether rich or poor, weak or strong.

2. National treatment: Treating foreigners and locals equally Imported and locally-produced goods should be treated equally — at least after the foreign goods have entered the market. The same should apply to foreign and domestic services, and to foreign and local trademarks, copyrights and patents. This principle of "national treatment" (giving others the same treatment as one's own nationals) is also found in all the three main WTO agreements (Article 3 of GATT, Article 17 of GATS and Article 3 of TRIPS), although once again the principle is handled slightly differently in each of these.

National treatment only applies once a product, service or item of intellectual property has entered the market. Therefore, charging customs duty on an import is not a violation of national treatment even if locally-produced products are not charged an equivalent tax.

Freer trade: gradually, through negotiation

Lowering trade barriers is one of the most obvious means of encouraging trade. The barriers concerned include customs duties (or tariffs) and measures such as import bans or quotas that restrict quantities selectively. From time to time other issues such as red tape and exchange rate policies have also been discussed.

Since GATT's creation in 1947-48 there have been eight rounds of trade negotiations. A ninth round, under the Doha Development Agenda, is now underway. At first these focused on lowering tariffs (customs duties) on imported goods. As a result of the negotiations, by the mid-1990s industrial countries' tariff rates on industrial goods had fallen steadily to less than 4%.

But by the 1980s, the negotiations had expanded

to cover non-tariff barriers on goods, and to the new areas such as services and intellectual property.

Opening markets can be beneficial, but it also requires adjustment. The WTO agreements allow countries to introduce changes gradually, through "progressive liberalization". Developing countries are usually given longer to fulfil their obligations.

Predictability: through binding and transparency

Sometimes, promising not to raise a trade barrier can be as important as lowering one, because the promise gives businesses a clearer view of their future opportunities. With stability and predictability, investment is encouraged, jobs are created and consumers can fully enjoy the benefits of competition — choice and lower prices. The multilateral trading system is an attempt by governments to make the business environment stable and predictable.

The Uruguay Round

increased bindings

Percentages of tariffs bound before and after the 1986-94 talks

	Before	After
Developed countries	78	99
Developing countries	21	73

Transition economies	73	98

(These are tariff lines, so percentages are not weighted according to trade volume or value)

In the WTO, when countries agree to open their markets for goods or services, they "bind" their commitments. For goods, these bindings amount to ceilings on customs tariff rates. Sometimes countries tax imports at rates that are lower than the bound rates. Frequently this is the case in developing countries. In developed countries the rates actually charged and the bound rates tend to be the same.

A country can change its bindings, but only after negotiating with its trading partners, which could mean compensating them for loss of trade. One of the achievements of the Uruguay Round of multilateral trade talks was to increase the amount of trade under binding commitments (*see table*). In agriculture, 100% of products now have bound tariffs. The result of all this: a substantially higher degree of market security for traders and investors.

The system tries to improve predictability and stability in other ways as well. One way is to discourage the use of quotas and other measures used to set limits on quantities of imports — administering quotas can lead to more red-tape and accusations of unfair play. Another is to make countries' trade rules as clear and public ("transparent") as possible. Many WTO agreements require governments to disclose their policies and practices publicly within the country or by notifying the WTO. The regular surveillance of national trade policies through the provides a further means of encouraging transparency both domestically and at the multilateral level.

Promoting fair competition

The WTO is sometimes described as a "free trade" institution, but that is not entirely accurate. The system does allow tariffs and, in limited circumstances, other forms of protection. More accurately, it is a system of rules dedicated to open, fair and undistorted competition.

The rules on non-discrimination — MFN and national treatment — are designed to secure fair conditions of trade. So too are those on dumping (exporting at below cost to gain market share) and subsidies. The issues are complex, and the rules try to establish what is fair or unfair, and how governments can respond, in particular by charging additional import duties calculated to compensate for damage caused by unfair trade.

Many of the other WTO agreements aim to support fair competition: in agriculture, intellectual property, services, for example. The agreement on government procurement (a "plurilateral" agreement because it is signed by only a few WTO members) extends competition rules to purchases by thousands of government entities in many countries. And so on.

Encouraging development and economic reform

The WTO system contributes to development. On the other hand, developing countries need flexibility in the time they take to implement the system's agreements. And the agreements themselves inherit the earlier provisions of GATT that allow for special assistance and trade concessions for developing countries.

Over three quarters of WTO members are developing countries and countries in transition to market economies. During the seven and a half years of the Uruguay Round, over 60 of these countries implemented trade liberalization programmes autonomously. At the same time, developing countries and transition economies were much more active and influential in the Uruguay Round negotiations than in any previous round, and they are even more so in the current Doha Development Agenda.

At the end of the Uruguay Round, developing countries were prepared to take on most of the obligations that are required of developed countries. But the agreements did give them transition periods to adjust to the more unfamiliar and, perhaps, difficult WTO provisions — particularly so for the poorest, "least-developed" countries. A ministerial decision adopted at the end of the round says better-off countries should accelerate implementing market access commitments on goods exported by the least-developed countries, and it seeks increased technical assistance for them. More recently, developed countries have started to allow duty-free and quota-free imports for almost all products from least-developed countries. On all of this, the WTO and its members are still going through a learning process. The current Doha Development Agenda includes developing countries' concerns about the difficulties they face in implementing the Uruguay Round agreements.

Chapter 3

Open Trade

The principles

The trading

system should be ... **without discrimination** — a country should not discriminate between its trading partners (giving them equally "most-favoured-nation" or

MFN status); and it should not discriminate between its own and foreign products, services or nationals (giving them "national treatment");

freer

— barriers coming down through negotiation;

predictable — foreign companies, investors and governments should be confident that trade barriers (including tariffs and non-tariff barriers) should not be raised arbitrarily; tariff rates and market-opening commitments are "bound" in the WTO;

more competitive — discour

aging "unfair" practices such as export subsidies and dumping products at below cost to gain market share; **more beneficial for less developed countri** es — giving them more time to adjust, greater flexibility, and special privileges.

Why 'most-favoured'?

This sounds like a contradiction. It suggests special treatment, but in the WTO it actually means non-discrimination — treating virtually everyone equally.

This is what happens. Each member treats all the other members equally as "most-favoured" trading partners. If a country improves the benefits that it gives to one trading partner, it has to give the same "best" treatment to all the other WTO members so that they all remain "most-favoured".

Most-favoured nation (MFN) status did not always mean equal treatment. The first bilateral MFN treaties set up exclusive clubs among a country's "most-favoured" trading partners. Under GATT and now the WTO, the MFN club is no longer exclusive. The MFN principle ensures that each country treats its over—140 fellow-members equally.

But there are some exceptions ...

The data show a definite statistical link between freer trade and economic growth. Economic theory points to strong reasons for the link. All countries, including the poorest, have assets — human, industrial, natural, financial — which they can employ to produce goods and services for their domestic markets or to compete overseas. Economics tells us that we can benefit when these goods and services are traded. Simply put, the principle of "comparative advantage" says that countries prosper first by taking advantage of their assets in order to concentrate on what they can produce best, and then by trading these products for products that other countries produce best.

In other words, liberal trade policies — policies that allow the unrestricted flow of goods and services — sharpen competition, motivate innovation and breed success. They multiply the rewards that result from producing the best products, with the best design, at the best price.

But success in trade is not static. The ability to compete well in particular products can shift from company to company when the market changes or new technologies make cheaper and better products possible. Producers are encouraged to adapt gradually and in a relatively painless way. They can focus on new products, find a new "niche" in their current area or expand into new areas.

Experience shows that competitiveness can also shift between whole countries. A country that may have enjoyed an advantage because of lower labour costs or because it had good supplies of some natural resources, could also become uncompetitive in some goods or services as its economy develops. However, with the stimulus of an open economy, the country can move on to become competitive in some other goods or services. This is normally a gradual process.

Nevertheless, the temptation to ward off the challenge of competitive imports is always present. And richer governments are more likely to yield to the siren call of protectionism, for short term political gain — through subsidies, complicated red tape, and hiding behind legitimate policy objectives such as environmental preservation or consumer protection as an excuse to protect producers.

Protection ultimately leads to bloated, inefficient producers supplying consumers with outdated, unattractive products. In the end, factories close and jobs are lost despite the protection and subsidies. If other governments around the world pursue the same policies, markets contract and world economic activity is reduced. One of the objectives that governments bring to WTO negotiations is to prevent such a self-defeating and destructive drift into protectionism.

>

TRUE AND NON-TRIVIAL?

Nobel laureate Paul Samuelson was once challenged by the mathematician Stanislaw Ulam to "name me one proposition in all of the social sciences which is both true and non-trivial."

Samuelson's answer? Comparative advantage.

"That it is logically true need not be argued before a mathematician; that it is not trivial is attested by the thousands of important and intelligent men who have never been able to grasp the doctrine for themselves or to believe it after it was explained to them."

Comparative advantage

This is arguably the single most powerful insight into economics.

Suppose country A is better than country B at making automobiles, and country B is better than country A at making bread. It is obvious (the academics would say "trivial") that both would benefit if A specialized in automobiles, B specialized in bread and they traded their products. That is a case of **absolute advantage**.

But what if a country is bad at making everything? Will trade drive all producers out of business? The answer, according to Ricardo, is no. The reason is the principle of **comparative advantage**.

It says, countries A and B still stand to benefit from trading with each other even if A is better than B at making everything. If A is much more superior at making automobiles and only slightly superior at making bread, then A should still invest resources in what it does best — producing automobiles — and export the product to B. B should still invest in what it does best — making bread — and export that product to A, even if it is not as efficient as A. Both would still benefit from the trade. A country does not have to be best at anything to gain from trade. That is comparative advantage.

The theory dates back to classical economist David Ricardo. It is one of the most widely accepted among economists. It is also one of the most misunderstood among non-economists because it is confused with absolute advantage.

It is often claimed, for example, that some countries have no comparative advantage in anything. That is virtually impossible.

Think about it ...

Chapter 4

Development of GATT

Much of the history of those 47 years was written in Geneva. But it also traces a journey that spanned the continents, from that hesitant start in 1948 in Havana (Cuba), via Annecy (France), Torquay (UK), Tokyo (Japan), Punta del Este (Uruguay), Montreal (Canada), Brussels (Belgium) and finally to Marrakesh (Morocco) in 1994. During that period, the trading system came under GATT, salvaged from the aborted attempt to create the ITO. GATT helped establish a strong and prosperous multilateral trading system that became more and more liberal through . But by the 1980s the system needed a thorough overhaul. This led to the , and ultimately to the WTO.

GATT: 'provisional' for almost half a century

From 1948 to 1994, the General Agreement on Tariffs and Trade (GATT) provided the rules for much of world trade and presided over periods that saw some of the highest growth rates in international commerce. It seemed well-established, but throughout those 47 years, it was a provisional agreement and organization.

The original intention was to create a third institution to handle the trade side of international economic cooperation, joining the two "Bretton Woods" institutions, the World Bank and the International Monetary Fund. Over 50 countries participated in negotiations to create an International Trade Organization (ITO) as a specialized agency of the United Nations. The draft ITO Charter was ambitious. It extended beyond world trade disciplines, to include rules on employment, commodity agreements, restrictive business practices, international investment, and services. The aim was to create the ITO at a UN Conference on

Trade and Employment in Havana, Cuba in 1947.

Meanwhile, 15 countries had begun talks in December 1945 to reduce and bind customs tariffs. With the Second World War only recently ended, they wanted to give an early boost to trade liberalization, and to begin to correct the legacy of protectionist measures which remained in place from the early 1930s.

This first round of negotiations resulted in a package of trade rules and 45,000 tariff concessions affecting $10 billion of trade, about one fifth of the world's total. The group had expanded to 23 by the time the deal was signed on 30 October 1947. The tariff concessions came into effect by 30 June 1948 through a "Protocol of Provisional Application". And so the new General Agreement on Tariffs and Trade was born, with 23 founding members (officially "contracting parties").

The 23 were also part of the larger group negotiating the ITO Charter. One of the provisions of GATT says that they should accept some of the trade rules of the draft. This, they believed, should be done swiftly and "provisionally" in order to protect the value of the tariff concessions they had negotiated. They spelt out how they envisaged the relationship between GATT and the ITO Charter, but they also allowed for the possibility that the ITO might not be created. They were right.

The Havana conference began on 21 November 1947, less than a month after GATT was signed. The ITO Charter was finally agreed in Havana in March 1948, but ratification in some national legislatures proved impossible. The most serious opposition was in the US Congress, even though the US government had been one of the driving forces. In 1950, the United States government announced that it would not seek Congressional ratification of the Havana Charter, and the ITO was effectively dead. So, the GATT became the only multilateral instrument governing international trade from 1948 until the WTO was established in 1995.

For almost half a century, the GATT's basic legal principles remained much as they were in 1948. There were additions in the form of a section on development added in the 1960s and "" agreements (i.e. with voluntary membership) in the 1970s, and efforts to reduce tariffs further continued. Much of this was achieved through a series of multilateral negotiations known as "trade rounds" — the biggest leaps forward in international trade liberalization have come through these rounds which were held under GATT's auspices.

In the early years, the GATT trade rounds concentrated on further reducing tariffs. Then, the Kennedy Round in the mid-sixties brought about a GATT Anti-Dumping Agreement and a section on development. The Tokyo Round during the seventies was the first major attempt to tackle trade barriers that do not take the form of tariffs, and to improve the system. The eighth, the Uruguay Round of 1986-94, was the last and most extensive of all. It led to the WTO and a new set of agreements.

Chapter 5

Uruguay round

The trade chiefs

The Directors-general of GATT and WTO
· Sir Eric Wyndham-White (UK) 1948-68
· Olivier Long (Switzerland) 1968-80
· Arthur Dunkel (Switzerland) 1980-93
· Peter Sutherland (Ireland) GATT 1993-94; WTO 1995
· Renato Ruggiero (Italy) 1995-1999
· Mike Moore (New Zealand) 1999-2002
· Supachai Panitchpakdi (Thailand) 2002-2005
· Pascal Lamy (France) 2005–

GATT trade rounds

Year	Place/name	Subjects covered	Countries
1947	Geneva	Tariffs	23

Year	Round	Subjects	Countries
1949	Annecy	Tariffs	13
1951	Torquay	Tariffs	38
1956	Geneva	Tariffs	26
1960-1961	Geneva Dillon Round	Tariffs	26
1964-1967	Geneva Kennedy Round	Tariffs and anti-dumping measures	62
1973-1979	Geneva Tokyo Round	Tariffs, non-tariff measures, "framework" agreements	102

| 1986-1994 | Geneva | Uruguay Round | Tariffs, non-tariff measures, rules, services, intellectual property, dispute settlement, textiles, agriculture, creation of WTO, etc | 123 |

The

Tokyo Round 'codes'

Subsidies and countervailing measures — interpreting Articles 6, 16 and 23 of GATT

Technical barriers to trade — sometimes called

the Standards Code

Import licensing procedures

Government procurement

Customs valuation — interpreting Article 7

Anti-dumping —

interpreting Article 6, replacing the Kennedy Round code

Bovine Meat Arrangement

International Dairy Arrangement

Trade in Civil Aircraft

The Tokyo Round: a first try to reform the system

The Tokyo Round lasted from 1973 to 1979, with 102 countries participating. It continued GATT's efforts to progressively reduce tariffs. The results included an average one-third cut in customs duties in the world's nine major industrial markets, bringing the average tariff on industrial products down to 4.7%. The tariff reductions, phased in over a period of eight years, involved an element of "harmonization" — the higher the tariff, the larger the cut, proportionally.

In other issues, the Tokyo Round had mixed results. It failed to come to grips with the fundamental problems affecting farm trade and also stopped short of providing a modified agreement on "safeguards" (emergency import measures). Nevertheless, a series of agreements on non-tariff barriers did emerge from the negotiations, in some cases interpreting existing GATT rules, in others breaking entirely new ground. In most cases, only a relatively small number of (mainly industrialized) GATT members subscribed to these agreements and arrangements. Because they were not accepted by the full GATT membership, they were often informally called "codes".

They were not multilateral, but they were a beginning. Several codes were eventually amended in the Uruguay Round and turned into multilateral commitments accepted by all WTO members. Only four remained "plurilateral" — those on government procurement, bovine meat, civil aircraft and dairy products. In 1997 WTO members agreed to terminate the bovine meat and dairy agreements, leaving only two.

Did GATT succeed?

GATT was provisional with a limited field of action, but its success over 47 years in promoting and securing the liberalization of much of world trade is incontestable. Continual reductions in tariffs alone helped spur very high rates of world trade growth during the 1950s and 1960s — around 8% a year on average. And the momentum of trade liberalization helped ensure that trade growth consistently out-paced production growth throughout the GATT era, a measure of countries' increasing ability to trade with each other and to reap the benefits of trade. The rush of new members during the Uruguay

Round demonstrated that the multilateral trading system was recognized as an anchor for development and an instrument of economic and trade reform.

But all was not well. As time passed new problems arose. The Tokyo Round in the 1970s was an attempt to tackle some of these but its achievements were limited. This was a sign of difficult times to come.

GATT's success in reducing tariffs to such a low level, combined with a series of economic recessions in the 1970s and early 1980s, drove governments to devise other forms of protection for sectors facing increased foreign competition. High rates of unemployment and constant factory closures led governments in Western Europe and North America to seek bilateral market-sharing arrangements with competitors and to embark on a subsidies race to maintain their holds on agricultural trade. Both these changes undermined GATT's credibility and effectiveness.

The problem was not just a deteriorating trade policy environment. By the early 1980s the

General Agreement was clearly no longer as relevant to the realities of world trade as it had been in the 1940s. For a start, world trade had become far more complex and important than 40 years before: the globalization of the world economy was underway, trade in services — not covered by GATT rules — was of major interest to more and more countries, and international investment had expanded. The expansion of services trade was also closely tied to further increases in world merchandise trade. In other respects, GATT had been found wanting. For instance, in agriculture, loopholes in the multilateral system were heavily exploited, and efforts at liberalizing agricultural trade met with little success. In the textiles and clothing sector, an exception to GATT's normal disciplines was negotiated in the 1960s and early 1970s, leading to the . Even GATT's institutional structure and its dispute settlement system were causing concern.

These and other factors convinced GATT members that a new effort to reinforce and extend the multilateral system should be attempted. That effort resulted in the , the

Marrakesh Declaration, and the creation of the WTO.

The seeds of the Uruguay Round were sown in November 1982 at a ministerial meeting of GATT members in Geneva. Although the ministers intended to launch a major new negotiation, the conference stalled on agriculture and was widely regarded as a failure. In fact, the work programme that the ministers agreed formed the basis for what was to become the Uruguay Round negotiating agenda.

Nevertheless, it took four more years of exploring, clarifying issues and painstaking consensus-building, before ministers agreed to launch the new round. They did so in September 1986, in Punta del Este, Uruguay. They eventually accepted a negotiating agenda that covered virtually every outstanding trade policy issue. The talks were going to extend the trading system into several new areas, notably trade in services and intellectual property, and to reform trade in the sensitive sectors of agriculture and textiles. All the original GATT articles were up for review. It was the biggest negotiating mandate on trade ever agreed, and the ministers gave themselves four years to complete it.

Two years later, in December 1988, ministers met again in Montreal, Canada, for what was supposed to be an assessment of progress at the round's half-way point. The purpose was to clarify the agenda for the remaining two years, but the talks ended in a deadlock that was not resolved until officials met more quietly in Geneva the following April.

Despite the difficulty, during the Montreal meeting, ministers did agree a package of early results. These included some concessions on market access for tropical products — aimed at assisting developing countries — as well as a streamlined , and the which provided for the first comprehensive, systematic and regular reviews of national trade policies and practices of GATT members. The round was supposed to end when ministers met once more in Brussels, in December 1990. But they disagreed on how to reform agricultural trade and decided to extend the talks. The Uruguay Round entered its bleakest period.

Despite the poor political outlook, a considerable amount of technical work continued, leading to the first draft of a final legal agreement. This draft "Final Act" was compiled by the then GATT director-general, Arthur Dunkel, who chaired the negotiations at officials' level. It was put on the table in Geneva in December 1991. The text fulfilled every part of the Punta del Este mandate, with one exception — it did not contain the participating countries' lists of commitments for cutting import duties and opening their services markets. The draft became the basis for the final agreement.

Over the following two years, the negotiations lurched between impending failure, to predictions of imminent success. Several deadlines came and went. New points of major conflict emerged to join agriculture: services, market access, anti-dumping rules, and the proposed creation of a new institution.

Differences between the United States and European Union became central to hopes for a final, successful conclusion.

In November 1992, the US and EU settled most of their differences on agriculture in a deal known informally as the "Blair House accord". By July 1993 the "Quad" (US, EU, Japan and Canada) announced significant progress in negotiations on tariffs and related subjects ("market access"). It took until 15 December 1993 for every issue to be finally resolved and for negotiations on market access for goods and services to be concluded (although some final touches were completed in talks on market access a few weeks later). On 15 April 1994, the deal was signed by ministers from most of the 123 participating governments at a meeting in Marrakesh, Morocco.

The delay had some merits. It allowed some negotiations to progress further than would have been possible in 1990: for example some aspects of services and intellectual property, and the creation of the WTO itself. But the task had been immense, and negotiation-fatigue was felt in trade bureaucracies around the world. The difficulty of reaching agreement on a complete package containing almost the entire range of current trade issues led some to conclude that a negotiation on this scale would never again be possible. Yet, the Uruguay Round agreements contain timetables for new negotiations on a number of topics. And by 1996, some countries were openly calling for a new round early in the next century. The response was mixed; but the Marrakesh agreement did already include commitments to reopen negotiations on agriculture and services at the turn of the century. These began in early 2000 and were incorporated into the Doha Development Agenda in late 2001.

What happened to GATT?

The WTO replaced GATT as an international organization, but the General Agreement still exists as the WTO's umbrella treaty for trade in goods, updated as a result of the Uruguay Round negotiations. Trade lawyers distinguish between GATT 1994, the updated parts of GATT, and GATT 1947, the original agreement which is still the heart of GATT 1994. Confusing? For most of us, it's enough to refer simply to "GATT".

The post-Uruguay Round built-in agenda

Many of the Uruguay Round agreements set timetables for future work. Part of this "built-in agenda" started almost immediately. In some areas, it included new or further negotiations. In other areas, it included assessments or reviews of the situation at specified times. Some negotiations were quickly completed, notably in basic telecommunications, financial services. (Member governments also swiftly agreed a deal for freer trade in information technology products, an issue outside the "built-in agenda".)

The agenda originally built into the Uruguay Round agreements has seen additions and modifications. A number of items are now part of the Doha Agenda, some of them updated.

There were well over 30 items in the original built-in agenda. This is a selection of highlights:

1996

- Maritime services: market access

- negotiations to end (30 June 1996, suspended to 2000, now part of Doha Development Agenda)
- Services and environment: deadline for working party report (ministerial conference, December 1996)
- Government procurement of services: negotiations start

1997

- Basic telecoms: negotiations end (15 February)
- Financial services: negotiations end (30 December)
- Intellectual property, creating a multilateral system of notification and registration of geographical indications for wines: negotiations start, now part of Doha Development Agenda

1998

- Textiles and clothing: new phase begins 1 January
- Services (emergency safeguards): results of

negotiations on emergency safeguards to take effect (by 1 January 1998, deadline now March 2004)

- Rules of origin: Work programme on harmonization of rules of origin to be completed (20 July 1998)
- Government procurement: further negotiations start, for improving rules and procedures (by end of 1998)
- Dispute settlement: full review of rules and procedures (to start by end of 1998)

1999

- Intellectual property: certain exceptions to patentability and protection of plant varieties: review starts

2000

- Agriculture: negotiations start, now part of Doha Development Agenda
- Services: new round of negotiations start, now part of Doha Development Agenda
- Tariff bindings: review of definition of "principle supplier" having negotiating

- rights under GATT Art 28 on modifying bindings
- Intellectual property: first of two-yearly reviews of the implementation of the agreement

2002

- Textiles and clothing: new phase begins 1 January

2005

- Textiles and clothing: full integration into GATT and agreement expires 1 January

These agreements are often called the WTO's trade rules, and the WTO is often described as "rules-based", a system based on rules. But it's important to remember that the rules are actually agreements that governments negotiated.

Chapter 6
WTO Agreements

This chapter focuses on the Uruguay Round agreements, which are the basis of the present WTO system. Additional work is also now underway in the WTO. This is the result of decisions taken at Ministerial Conferences, in particular the meeting in Doha, November 2001, when new negotiations and other work were launched. (More on the Doha Agenda, later.)

Six-part broad outline

The table of contents of "The Results of the Uruguay Round of Multilateral Trade Negotiations: The Legal Texts" is a daunting list of about 60 agreements, annexes, decisions and understandings. In fact, the agreements fall into a simple structure with six main parts: an umbrella agreement (the Agreement Establishing the WTO); agreements for each of the three broad areas of trade that the WTO covers (goods, services and intellectual property); dispute settlement; and reviews of governments' trade policies.

The agreements for the two largest areas — goods and services — share a common three-part outline, even though the detail is sometimes quite different.

They start with **broad principles**: the General Agreement on Tariffs and Trade (GATT) (for goods), and the General Agreement on Trade in Services (GATS). (The third area, Trade-Related Aspects of Intellectual Property Rights (TRIPS), also falls into this category although at present it has no additional parts.)

Then come **extra agreements and annexes** dealing with the special requirements of specific sectors or issues.

Finally, there are the detailed and lengthy **schedules (or lists) of commitments** made by individual countries allowing specific foreign products or service-providers access to their markets. For GATT, these take the form of

<u>binding commitments</u> on tariffs for goods in general, and combinations of tariffs and quotas for some agricultural goods. For GATS, the commitments state how much access foreign service providers are allowed for specific sectors, and they include lists of types of services where individual countries say they are not applying the "most-favoured-nation" principle of non-discrimination.

Underpinning these are dispute settlement, which is based on the agreements and commitments, and trade policy reviews, an exercise in transparency.

Much of the Uruguay Round dealt with the first two parts: general principles and principles for specific sectors. At the same time, market access negotiations were possible for industrial goods. Once the principles had been worked out, negotiations could proceed on the commitments for sectors such as agriculture and services.

In a nutshell

The basic structure of the WTO agreements:

how the six main areas fit together — the umbrella WTO Agreement, goods, services, intellectual property, disputes and trade policy reviews.

Umbrella **AGREEMEN**

	ESTABLISHING WTO		
	Goods	Services	Intellectual property
Basic principles	GATT	GATS	TRIPS
Additional details	Other goods agreements and annexes	Services annexes	
Market access commitments	Countries' schedules of commitments	Countries' schedules of commitments(a	

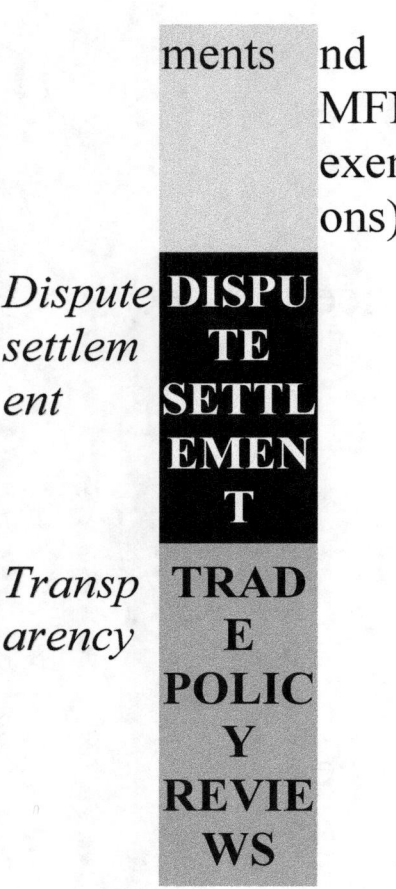

Additional agreements

Another group of agreements not included in the diagram is also important: the two not signed by all members: civil aircraft and government procurement.

Further changes on the horizon, the Doha Agenda

These agreements are not static; they are

renegotiated from time to time and new agreements can be added to the package. Many are now being negotiated under the Doha Development Agenda, launched by WTO trade ministers in Doha, Qatar, in November 2001

Developed countries' tariff cuts were for the most part phased in over five years from 1 January 1995. The result is a 40% cut in their tariffs on industrial products, from an average of 6.3% to 3.8%. The value of imported industrial products that receive duty-free treatment in developed countries will jump from 20% to 44%.

There will also be fewer products charged high duty rates. The proportion of imports into developed countries from all sources facing tariffs rates of more than 15% will decline from 7% to 5%. The proportion of developing country exports facing tariffs above 15% in industrial countries will fall from 9% to 5%.

The Uruguay Round package has been improved. On 26 March 1997, 40 countries accounting for more than 92% of world trade in , agreed to eliminate import duties and other charges on these products by 2000 (by 2005 in a handful of cases). As with other tariff commitments, each participating country is applying its commitments equally to exports from all WTO members (i.e. on a <u>most-favoured-nation</u> basis), even from members that did not make commitments.

More bindings

Developed countries increased the number of imports whose tariff rates are "" (committed and difficult to increase) from 78% of product lines to 99%. For developing countries, the increase was considerable: from 21% to 73%. Economies in transition from central planning increased their bindings from 73% to 98%. This all means a substantially higher degree of market security for traders and investors.

>

> See also

And agriculture ...

Tariffs on all agricultural products are now bound. Almost all import restrictions that did not take the form of tariffs, such as quotas, have been converted to tariffs — a process known as "tariffication". This has made markets substantially more predictable for agriculture. Previously more than 30% of agricultural produce had faced quotas or import restrictions. The first step in "tariffication" was to replace these restrictions with tariffs that represented about the same level of protection. Then, over six years from 1995-2000, these tariffs were gradually reduced (the reduction period for developing countries ends in 2005). The market access commitments on agriculture also eliminate previous import bans on certain products.

In addition, the lists include countries' commitments to reduce domestic support and export subsidies for agricultural products. (See section on .)

Chapter 7

Reducing Tariffs

What is this agreement called?

There is no legally binding agreement that sets out the targets for tariff reductions (e.g. by what percentage they were to be cut as a result of the Uruguay Round).

Instead, individual countries listed their commitments in schedules annexed to Marrakesh Protocol to the General Agreement on Tariffs and Trade 1994. This is the legally binding agreement for the reduced tariff rates. Since then, additional commitments were made under the 1997 Information Technology Agreement.

'Binding' tariffs

The market access schedules are not simply announcements of tariff rates. They represent commitments not to increas e tariffs above the listed rates — the rates are "bound". For developed countries, the bound rates are generally the rates actually charged. Most developing countries have bound the rates somewhat higher than the actual rates charged, so the bound rates serve as ceilings.

Countries can break a commitment (i.e. raise a

tariff above the bound rate), but only with difficulty. To do so they have to negotiate with the countries most concerned and that could result in compen sation for trading partners' loss of trade.

Chapter 8

Reforms in Agriculture

The Agriculture Agreement: new rules and commitments

The objective of the **Agriculture Agreement** is to reform trade in the sector and to make policies more market-oriented. This would improve predictability and security for importing and exporting countries alike.

The new rules and commitments apply to:

- **market access** — various trade restrictions confronting imports
- **domestic support** — subsidies and other programmes, including those that raise or guarantee farmgate prices and farmers' incomes
- **export subsidies** and other methods used to make exports artificially competitive.

The agreement does allow governments to support their rural economies, but preferably through policies that cause less distortion to trade. It also allows some flexibility in the way commitments are implemented. Developing countries do not have to cut their subsidies or lower their tariffs as much as developed countries, and they are given extra time to complete their obligations. Least-developed countries don't have to do this at all. Special provisions deal with the interests of countries that rely on imports for their food supplies, and the concerns of least-developed economies.

"Peace" provisions within the agreement aim to reduce the likelihood of disputes or challenges on agricultural subsidies over a period of nine years, until the end of 2003.

Market access: 'tariffs only', please

The new rule for market access in agricultural products is "tariffs only". Before the Uruguay Round, some agricultural imports were restricted by quotas and other non-tariff measures. These have been replaced by tariffs that provide more-or-less equivalent levels of protection — if the previous policy meant domestic prices were 75% higher than world prices, then the new tariff could be around 75%. (Converting the quotas and other types of measures to tariffs in this way was called "tariffication".)

Numerical targets for agriculture

The reductions in agricultural subsidies and protection agreed in the Uruguay Round. Only the figures for cutting export subsidies appear in the agreem ent.

	Developed countries 6 years: 1995-2000	Developing countries 10 years: 1995-2004
Tariffs		
average cut for all agricultural products	-36%	-24%
minimum cut per product	-15%	-10%
Domestic		

support total AMS cuts for sector (base period: 1986-88)	-20%	-13%
Exports value of subsidies	-36%	-24%
subsidized quantities (base period: 1986-90)	-21%	-14%

Least

developed countries do not have to make commitments to reduce tariffs or subsidies.

The base level for tariff cuts was the bound rate before

1 January 1995; or, for unbound tariffs, the actual rate charged in September 1986 when the Uruguay Round began. The other figures were

targets used to calculate countries' legally-binding "schedules" of commitments.

The tariffication package contained more. It ensured that quantities imported before the agreement took effect could continue to be imported, and it guaranteed that some new quantities were charged duty rates that were not prohibitive. This was achieved by a system of "" — lower tariff rates for specified quantities, higher (sometimes much higher) rates for quantities that exceed the quota.

The newly committed tariffs and tariff quotas, covering all agricultural products, took effect in 1995. Uruguay Round participants agreed that developed countries would cut the tariffs (the higher out-of-quota rates in the case of tariff-quotas) by an average of 36%, in equal steps over six years. Developing countries would make 24% cuts over 10 years. Several developing countries also used the option of offering ceiling tariff rates in cases where duties were not "bound" (i.e. committed under GATT or WTO regulations) before the Uruguay Round. Least-developed countries do not have to cut their tariffs. (These figures do not actually appear in the Agriculture Agreement. Participants used them to prepare their schedules — i.e. lists of commitments. It is the commitments listed in the schedules that are legally binding.)

For products whose non-tariff restrictions have been converted to tariffs, governments are allowed to take special emergency actions ("special safeguards") in order to prevent swiftly falling prices or surges in imports from hurting their farmers. But the agreement specifies when and how those emergency actions can be introduced (for example, they cannot be used on imports within a tariff-quota).

Four countries used "special treatment" provisions to restrict imports of particularly sensitive products (mainly rice) during the implementation period (to 2000 for developed countries, to 2004 for developing nations), but subject to strictly defined conditions, including minimum access for overseas suppliers. The four were: Japan, Rep. of Korea, and the Philippines for rice; and Israel for sheepmeat, wholemilk powder and certain cheeses. Japan and Israel have now given up this right, but Rep. of Korea and the Philippines have extended their special treatment for rice. A new member, Chinese Taipei, gave special treatment to rice in its first year of membership, 2002.

Domestic support: some you can, some you can't

The main complaint about policies which support domestic prices, or subsidize production in some other way, is that they encourage over-production. This squeezes out imports or leads to export subsidies and low-priced dumping on world markets. The Agriculture Agreement distinguishes between support programmes that stimulate production directly, and those that are considered to have no direct effect.

Domestic policies that do have a direct effect on production and trade have to be cut back. WTO members calculated how much support of this kind they were providing per year for the agricultural sector (using calculations known as "total aggregate measurement of support" or "Total AMS") in the base years of 1986-88. Developed countries agreed to reduce these figures by 20% over six years starting in 1995. Developing countries agreed to make 13% cuts over 10 years. Least-developed countries do not need to make any cuts. (This category of domestic support is sometimes called the "amber box", a reference to the amber colour of traffic lights, which means "slow down".)

Measures with minimal impact on trade can be used freely — they are in a "green box" ("green" as in traffic lights). They include government services such as research, disease control, infrastructure and food security. They also include payments made directly to farmers that do not stimulate production, such as certain forms of direct income support, assistance to help farmers restructure agriculture, and direct payments under environmental and regional assistance programmes.

Also permitted, are certain direct payments to

farmers where the farmers are required to limit production (sometimes called "blue box" measures), certain government assistance programmes to encourage agricultural and rural development in developing countries, and other support on a small scale ("de minimis") when compared with the total value of the product or products supported (5% or less in the case of developed countries and 10% or less for developing countries).

Export subsidies: limits on spending and quantities

The Agriculture Agreement prohibits export subsidies on agricultural products unless the subsidies are specified in a member's lists of commitments. Where they are listed, the agreement requires WTO members to cut both the amount of money they spend on export subsidies and the quantities of exports that receive subsidies. Taking averages for 1986-90 as the base level, developed countries agreed to cut the value of export subsidies by 36% over the six years starting in 1995 (24% over 10 years for developing countries). Developed countries also agreed to reduce the quantities of subsidized exports by 21% over the six years (14% over 10 years for developing countries). Least-developed countries do not need to make any cuts.

During the six-year implementation period, developing countries are allowed under certain conditions to use subsidies to reduce the costs of marketing and transporting exports.

The least-developed and those depending on food imports

Under the Agriculture Agreement, WTO members have to reduce their subsidized exports. But some importing countries depend on supplies of cheap, subsidized food from the major industrialized nations. They include some of the poorest countries, and although their farming sectors might receive a boost from higher prices caused by reduced export subsidies, they might need temporary assistance to make the necessary adjustments to deal with higher priced imports, and eventually to export. A special ministerial decision sets out objectives, and certain measures, for the provision of food aid and aid for agricultural development. It also refers to the possibility of assistance from the International Monetary Fund and the World Bank to finance commercial food imports.

Problem: How do you ensure that your country's consumers are being supplied with food that is safe to eat — "safe" by the standards you consider appropriate? And at the same time, how can you ensure that strict health and safety regulations are not being used as an excuse for protecting domestic producers?

A separate agreement on food safety and animal and plant health standards (the **Sanitary and Phytosanitary Measures Agreement** or **SPS**) sets out the basic rules.

It allows countries to set their own standards. But it also says regulations must be based on science. They should be applied only to the extent necessary to protect human, animal or plant life or health. And they should not arbitrarily or unjustifiably discriminate between countries where identical or similar conditions prevail.

Member countries are encouraged to use international standards, guidelines and recommendations where they exist. When they do, they are unlikely to be challenged legally in a WTO dispute. However, members may use measures which result in higher standards if there is scientific justification. They can also set higher standards based on appropriate assessment of risks so long as the approach is consistent, not arbitrary. And they can to some extent apply the "precautionary principle", a kind of "safety first" approach to deal with scientific uncertainty. Article 5.7 of the SPS Agreement allows temporary "precautionary" measures.

The agreement still allows countries to use different standards and different methods of inspecting products. So how can an exporting country be sure the practices it applies to its products are acceptable in an importing country? If an exporting country can demonstrate that the measures it applies to its exports achieve the same level of health protection as in the importing country, then the importing country is expected to accept the exporting country's standards and methods.

The agreement includes provisions on control, inspection and approval procedures. Governments must provide advance notice of new or changed sanitary and phytosanitary regulations, and establish a national enquiry point to provide information. The agreement complements that on technical barriers to trade.

>

Technical regulations and standards

Technical regulations and standards are important, but they vary from country to country. Having too many different standards makes life difficult for producers and exporters. If the standards are set arbitrarily, they could be used as an excuse for protectionism. Standards can become obstacles to trade. But they are also necessary for a range of reasons, from environmental protection, safety, national security to consumer information. And they can help trade. Therefore the same basic question arises again: how to ensure that standards are genuinely useful, and not arbitrary or an excuse for protectionism.

Chapter 9

Technical Barriers to Trade, Textiles

The **Technical Barriers to Trade Agreement (TBT)** tries to ensure that regulations, standards, testing and certification procedures do not create unnecessary obstacles.

However, the agreement also recognizes countries' rights to adopt the standards they consider appropriate — for example, for human, animal or plant life or health, for the protection of the environment or to meet other consumer interests. Moreover, members are not prevented from taking measures necessary to ensure their standards are met. But that is counterbalanced with disciplines. A myriad of regulations can be a nightmare for manufacturers and exporters. Life can be simpler if governments apply international standards, and the agreement encourages them to do so In any case, whatever regulations they use should not discriminate.

The agreement also sets out a code of good practice for both governments and non-governmental or industry bodies to prepare, adopt and apply voluntary standards. Over 200 standards-setting bodies apply the code.

The agreement says the procedures used to decide whether a product conforms with relevant standards have to be fair and equitable. It discourages any methods that would give domestically produced goods an unfair advantage. The agreement also encourages countries to recognize each other's procedures for assessing whether a product conforms. Without recognition, products might have to be tested twice, first by the exporting country and then by the importing country.

Manufacturers and exporters need to know what the latest standards are in their prospective markets. To help ensure that this information is made available conveniently, all WTO member governments are required to establish national enquiry points and to keep each other informed through the WTO — around 900 new or changed regulations are notified each year. The Technical Barriers to Trade Committee is the major clearing house for members to share the information and the major forum to discuss concerns about the regulations and their implementation.

From 1974 until the end of the Uruguay Round, the trade was governed by the Multifibre Arrangement (MFA). This was a framework for bilateral agreements or unilateral actions that established quotas limiting imports into countries whose domestic industries were facing serious damage from rapidly increasing imports.

The quotas were the most visible feature. They conflicted with GATT's general preference for customs tariffs instead of measures that restrict quantities. They were also exceptions to the GATT principle of treating all trading partners equally because they specified how much the importing country was going to accept from individual exporting countries.

Since 1995, the WTO's <u>Agreement on Textiles and Clothing (ATC)</u> took over from the Mulltifibre Arrangement. By 1 January 2005, the sector was fully integrated into normal GATT rules. In particular, the quotas came to an end, and importing countries are no longer be able to discriminate between exporters. The Agreement on Textiles and Clothing no longer exists: it's the only WTO agreement that had self-destruction built in.

Integration: returning products gradually to GATT rules

Textiles and clothing products were returned to GATT rules over the 10-year period. This happened gradually, in four steps, to allow time for both importers and exporters to adjust to the new situation. Some of these products were previously under quotas. Any quotas that were in place on 31 December 1994 were carried over into the new agreement. For products that had quotas, the result of integration into GATT was the removal of these quotas.

The agreement stated the percentage of products that had to be brought under GATT rules at each step. If any of these products came under quotas, then the quotas had to be removed at the same time. The percentages were applied to the importing country's textiles and clothing trade levels in 1990. The agreement also said the quantities of imports permitted under the quotas had to grow annually, and that the rate of expansion had to increase at each stage. How fast that expansion would be was set out in a formula based on the growth rate that existed under the old Multifibre Arrangement (*see table*).

Four steps over 10 years

The schedule for freeing textiles and garments products from import quotas (and returnin g them to GATT rules), and how fast remaining quotas had to be expanded.

The example is based on the commonly-used 6% annual expansi

on rate of the old Multifibre Arrangement. In practice, the rates used under the MFA varied from product to product.

Step	Percentage of products	Percentage of products

	to be brought under GATT (including removal of any quotas)	to be brought under GATT (including removal of any quotas)
Step 1: 1 Jan 1995 (to 31 Dec 1997)	**16%** (minimum, taking 1990 imports as base)	**6.96%** per year
Step 2: 1 Jan 1998 (to 31 Dec 2001)	**17%**	**8.7%** per year
Step 3: 1 Jan	**18%**	**11.05%**

	2002 (to 31 Dec 2004)		per year
Step 4: 1 Jan 2005	**49%** (maximum)		**No quotas left**

>*Full integration into GATT (and final elimination of quotas).*

>*Agreement on Textiles and Clothing termina*

tes.

The actual formula for import growth under quotas was: by *0.1* x *pre-1995 growth rate* in the first step; *0.25* x *Step 1 growth rate* in the second step; and

0.27 x Step 2 growth rate in the third step.

Products brought under GATT rules at each of the first three stages had to cover the four main types of textiles and clothing: tops and yarns; fabrics; made-up textile products; and clothing. Any other restrictions that did not come under the Multifibre Arrangement and did not conform with regular WTO agreements by 1996 had to be made to conform or be phased out by 2005.

If further cases of damage to the industry arose during the transition, the agreement allowed additional restrictions to be imposed temporarily under strict conditions. These "transitional safeguards" were not the same as the safeguard measures normally allowed under GATT because they can be applied on imports from specific exporting countries. But the importing country had to show that its domestic industry was suffering serious damage or was threatened with serious damage. And it had to show that the damage was the result of two things: increased imports of the product in question from all sources, and a sharp and substantial increase from the specific exporting country. The safeguard restriction could be implemented either by mutual agreement following consultations, or unilaterally. It was subject to review by the .

In any system where quotas are set for individual exporting countries, exporters might try to get around the quotas by shipping products through third countries or making false declarations about the products' country of origin. The agreement included provisions to cope with these cases.

The agreement envisaged special treatment for certain categories of countries — for example, new market entrants, small suppliers, and least-developed countries.

A **Textiles Monitoring Body (TMB)** supervised the agreement's implementation. It consisted of a chairman and 10 members acting in their personal capacity. It monitored actions taken under the agreement to ensure that they were consistent, and it reported to the Goods Council which reviewed the operation of the agreement before each new step of the integration process. The Textiles Monitoring Body also dealt with disputes under the Agreement on Textiles and Clothing. If they remained unresolved, the disputes could be brought to the WTO's regular Dispute Settlement Body. When the Textiles and Clothing Agreement expired on 1 January 2005, the Textiles Monitoring Body also ceased to exist

Chapter 10
GATS

Services represent the fastest growing sector of the global economy and account for two thirds of global output, one third of global employment and nearly 20% of global trade.

When the idea of bringing rules on services into the multilateral trading system was floated in the early to mid 1980s, a number of countries were sceptical and even opposed. They believed such an agreement could undermine governments' ability to pursue national policy objectives and constrain their regulatory powers. The agreement that was developed, however, allows a high degree of flexibility, both within the framework of rules and also in terms of the market access commitments.

GATS explained

The **General Agreement on Trade in Services** has three elements: the main text containing general obligations and disciplines; annexes dealing with rules for specific sectors; and individual countries' specific commitments to provide access to their markets, including indications of where countries are temporarily not applying the "most-favoured-nation" principle of non-discrimination.

General obligations and disciplines

Total coverage The agreement covers all internationally-traded services — for example, banking, telecommunications, tourism, professional services, etc. It also defines four ways (or "modes") of trading services:

services supplied from one country to another (e.g. international telephone calls), officially known as **"cross-border supply"** (in WTO jargon, "mode 1")

consumers or firms making use of a service in another country (e.g. tourism), officially **"consumption abroad"** ("mode 2")

a foreign company setting up subsidiaries or branches to provide services in another country (e.g. foreign banks setting up operations in a country), officially **"commercial presence"** ("mode 3")

individuals travelling from their own country to supply services in another (e.g. fashion models or consultants), officially **"presence of natural persons"** ("mode 4")

Most-favoured-nation (MFN) treatment
Favour one, favour all. MFN means treating one's trading partners equally on the principle of non-discrimination. Under GATS, if a country allows foreign competition in a sector, equal opportunities in that sector should be given to service providers from all other WTO members. (This applies even if the country has

made no specific commitment to provide foreign companies access to its markets under the WTO.)

MFN applies to all services, but some special temporary exemptions have been allowed. When GATS came into force, a number of countries already had preferential agreements in services that they had signed with trading partners, either bilaterally or in small groups. WTO members felt it was necessary to maintain these preferences temporarily. They gave themselves the right to continue giving more favourable treatment to particular countries in particular services activities by listing "MFN exemptions" alongside their first sets of commitments. In order to protect the general MFN principle, the exemptions could only be made once; nothing can be added to the lists. They are currently being reviewed as mandated, and will normally last no more than ten years.

Commitments on market access and national treatment Individual countries' commitments to open markets in specific sectors — and how open those markets will be — are the outcome of negotiations. The commitments appear in "schedules" that list the sectors being opened, the extent of market access being given in those sectors (e.g. whether there are any restrictions on foreign ownership), and any limitations on national treatment (whether some rights granted to local companies will not be granted to foreign companies). So, for example, if a government commits itself to allow foreign banks to operate in its domestic market, that is a **market-access commitment**. And if the government limits the number of licences it will issue, then that is a **market-access limitation**. If it also says foreign banks are only allowed one branch while domestic banks are allowed numerous branches, that is an **exception to the national treatment** principle.

These clearly defined commitments are "<u>bound</u>": like bound tariffs for trade in goods, they can only be modified after negotiations with affected countries. Because "unbinding" is difficult, the commitments are virtually guaranteed conditions for foreign exporters and importers of services and investors in the sector to do business.

Governmental services are explicitly carved out of the agreement and there is nothing in GATS that forces a government to privatize service industries. In fact the word "privatize" does not even appear in GATS. Nor does it outlaw government or even private monopolies.

The carve-out is an explicit commitment by WTO governments to allow publicly funded services in core areas of their responsibility. Governmental services are defined in the agreement as those that are not supplied commercially and do not compete with other suppliers. These services are not subject to any GATS disciplines, they are not covered by the negotiations, and commitments on market access and national treatment (treating foreign and domestic companies equally) do not apply to them.

GATS' approach to making commitments means that members are not obliged to do so on the whole universe of services sectors. A government may not want to make a commitment on the level of foreign competition in a given sector, because it considers the sector to be a core governmental function or indeed for any other reason. In this case, the government's only obligations are minimal, for example to be transparent in regulating the sector, and not to discriminate between foreign suppliers.

Transparency GATS says governments must

publish all relevant laws and regulations, and set up enquiry points within their bureaucracies. Foreign companies and governments can then use these inquiry points to obtain information about regulations in any service sector. And they have to notify the WTO of any changes in regulations that apply to the services that come under specific commitments.

Regulations: objective and reasonable Since domestic regulations are the most significant means of exercising influence or control over services trade, the agreement says governments should regulate services reasonably, objectively and impartially. When a government makes an administrative decision that affects a service, it should also provide an impartial means for reviewing the decision (for example a tribunal).

GATS does not require any service to be deregulated. Commitments to liberalize do not affect governments' right to set levels of quality, safety, or price, or to introduce regulations to pursue any other policy objective they see fit. A commitment to national treatment, for example, would only mean that the same regulations would apply to foreign suppliers as to nationals. Governments naturally retain their right to set qualification requirements for doctors or lawyers, and to set standards to ensure consumer health and safety.

Recognition When two (or more) governments have agreements recognizing each other's qualifications (for example, the licensing or certification of service suppliers), GATS says other members must also be given a chance to negotiate comparable pacts. The recognition of other countries' qualifications must not be discriminatory, and it must not amount to protectionism in disguise. These recognition agreements have to be notified to the WTO.

International payments and transfers Once a government has made a commitment to open a service sector to foreign competition, it must not normally restrict money being transferred out of the country as payment for services supplied ("current transactions") in that sector. The only exception is when there are balance-of-payments difficulties, and even then the restrictions must be temporary and subject to other limits and conditions.

Progressive liberalization The Uruguay Round was only the beginning. GATS requires more negotiations, which began in early 2000 and are now part of the Doha Development Agenda. The goal is to take the liberalization process further by increasing the level of commitments in schedules.

The annexes: services are not all the same

International trade in goods is a relatively simple idea to grasp: a product is transported from one country to another. Trade in services is much more diverse. Telephone companies, banks, airlines and accountancy firms provide their services in quite different ways. The GATS annexes reflect some of the diversity.

Movement of natural persons This annex deals with negotiations on individuals' rights to stay temporarily in a country for the purpose of providing a service. It specifies that the agreement does not apply to people seeking permanent employment or to conditions for obtaining citizenship, permanent residence or permanent employment.

Financial services Instability in the banking system affects the whole economy. The financial services annex gives governments very wide latitude to take prudential measures, such as those for the protection of investors, depositors and insurance policy holders, and to ensure the integrity and stability of the financial system. The annex also excludes from the agreement services provided when a government is exercising its authority over the financial system, for example central banks' services.

Telecommunications The telecommunications sector has a dual role: it is a distinct sector of economic activity; and it is an underlying means of supplying other economic activities (for example electronic money transfers). The annex says governments must ensure that foreign service suppliers are given access to the public telecommunications networks without discrimination.

Air transport services Under this annex, traffic rights and directly related activities are excluded from GATS's coverage. They are handled by other bilateral agreements. However, the annex establishes that the GATS will apply to aircraft repair and maintenance services, marketing of air transport services and computer-reservation services. Members are currently reviewing the annex.

Current work

GATS sets a heavy work programme covering a wide range of subjects. Work on some of the subjects started in 1995, as required, soon after GATS came into force in January 1995. Negotiations to further liberalize international trade in services started in 2000, along with other work involving study and review.

Negotiations (Article 19) Negotiations to further liberalize international trade in services started in early 2000 as mandated by GATS (Article 19).

The first phase of the negotiations ended successfully in March 2001 when members agreed on the guidelines and procedures for the negotiations, a key element in the negotiating mandate. By agreeing these guidelines, members set the objectives, scope and method for the negotiations in a clear and balanced manner.

They also unequivocally endorsed some of GATS' fundamental principles — i.e. members' right to regulate and to introduce new regulations on the supply of services in pursuit of national policy objectives; their right to specify which services they wish to open to foreign suppliers and under which conditions; and the overarching principle of flexibility for developing and least-developed countries. The guidelines are therefore sensitive to public policy concerns in important sectors such as health-care, public education and cultural industries, while stressing the importance of liberalization in general, and ensuring foreign service providers have effective access to domestic markets.

The 2001 Doha Ministerial Declaration incorporated these negotiations into the "single undertaking" of the Doha Development Agenda. Since July 2002, a process of bilateral negotiations on market access has been underway.

Work on GATS rules (Articles 10, 13, and 15)
Negotiations started in 1995 and are continuing

on the development of possible disciplines that are not yet included in GATS: rules on emergency safeguard measures, government procurement and subsidies. Work so far has concentrated on safeguards. These are temporary limitations on market access to deal with market disruption, and the negotiations aim to set up procedures and disciplines for governments using these. **Several deadlines have been missed. The current aim is for the results to come** into effect at the same time as those of the current services negotiations.

Work on domestic regulations (Article 6.4) Work started in 1995 to establish disciplines on domestic regulations — i.e. the requirements foreign service suppliers have to meet in order to operate in a market. The focus is on qualification requirements and procedures, technical standards and licensing requirements. By December 1998, members had agreed disciplines on domestic regulations for the accountancy sector. Since then, members have been engaged in developing general disciplines for all professional services and, where necessary, additional sectoral disciplines. All the agreed disciplines will be integrated into GATS and become legally binding by the end of the current services negotiations.

MFN exemptions (Annex on Article 2) Work on this subject started in 2000. When GATS came into force in 1995, members were allowed a once-only opportunity to take an exemption from the MFN principle of non-discrimination between a member's trading partners. The measure for which the exemption was taken is described in a member's MFN exemption list, indicating to which member the more favourable treatment applies, and specifying its duration. In principle, these exemptions should not last for more than ten years. As mandated by GATS, all these exemptions are currently being reviewed to examine whether the conditions which created the need for these exemptions in the first place still exist. And in any case, they are part of the current services negotiations.

Taking account of "autonomous" liberalization (Article 19) Countries that have liberalized on their own initiative since the last multilateral negotiations want that to be taken into account when they negotiate market access in services. The negotiating guidelines and procedures that members agreed in March 2001 for the GATS negotiations also call for criteria for taking this "autonomous" or unilateral liberalization into account. These were agreed on 6 March 2003.

Special treatment for least-developed

countries (Article 19) GATS mandates members to establish how to give special treatment to least-developed countries during the negotiations. (These "modalities" cover both the scope of the special treatment, and the methods to be used.) The least-developed countries began the discussions in March 2002. As a result of subsequent discussions, Members agreed the modalities on 3 September 2003.

Assessment of trade in services (Article 19) Preparatory work on this subject started in early 1999. GATS mandates that members assess trade in services, including the GATS objective of increasing the developing countries' participation in services trade. The negotiating guidelines reiterate this, requiring the negotiations to be adjusted in response to the assessment. Members generally acknowledge that the shortage of statistical information and other methodological problems make it impossible to conduct an assessment based on full data. However, they are continuing their discussions with the assistance of several papers produced by the Secretariat.

Air transport services At present, most of the air transport sector — traffic rights and services directly related to traffic rights — is excluded from GATS' coverage. However, GATS mandates a review by members of this situation. The purpose of the review, which started in early 2000, is to decide whether additional air transport services should be covered by GATS. The review could develop into a negotiation in its own right, resulting in an amendment of GATS itself by adding new services to its coverage and by adding specific commitments on these new services to national schedules.

Chapter 10

Intellectual Property

Ideas and knowledge are an increasingly important part of trade. Most of the value of new medicines and other high technology products lies in the amount of invention, innovation, research, design and testing involved. Films, music recordings, books, computer software and on-line services are bought and sold because of the information and creativity they contain, not usually because of the plastic, metal or paper used to make them. Many products that used to be traded as low-technology goods or commodities now contain a higher proportion of invention and design in their value — for example brandnamed clothing or new varieties of plants.

Creators can be given the right to prevent others from using their inventions, designs or other creations — and to use that right to negotiate payment in return for others using them. These are "intellectual property rights". They take a number of forms. For example books, paintings and films come under copyright; inventions can be patented; brandnames and product logos can be registered as trademarks; and so on. Governments and parliaments have given creators these rights as an incentive to produce ideas that will benefit society as a whole.

The extent of protection and enforcement of these rights varied widely around the world; and as intellectual property became more important in trade, these differences became a source of tension in international economic relations. New internationally-agreed trade rules for intellectual property rights were seen as a way to introduce more order and predictability, and for disputes to be settled more systematically.

The Uruguay Round achieved that. The WTO's TRIPS Agreement is an attempt to narrow the gaps in the way these rights are protected around the world, and to bring them under common international rules. It establishes minimum levels of protection that each government has to give to the intellectual property of fellow WTO members. In doing so, it strikes a balance between the long term benefits and possible short term costs to society. Society benefits in the long term when intellectual property protection encourages creation and invention, especially when the period of protection expires and the creations and inventions enter the public domain. Governments are allowed to reduce any short term costs through various exceptions, for example to tackle public health problems. And, when there are trade disputes over intellectual property rights, the WTO's dispute settlement system is now available.

The agreement covers five broad issues:

how basic principles of the trading system and other international intellectual property agreements should be applied

how to give adequate protection to intellectual property rights

how countries should enforce those rights adequately in their own territories

how to settle disputes on intellectual property between members of the WTO

special transitional arrangements during the period when the new system is being introduced.

Basic principles: national treatment, MFN, and balanced protection

As in GATT and GATS, the starting point of the intellectual property agreement is basic principles. And as in the two other agreements, non-discrimination features prominently:

<u>national treatment</u> (treating one's own nationals and foreigners equally), and <u>most-favoured-nation</u> treatment (equal treatment for nationals of all trading partners in the WTO). National treatment is also a key principle in other intellectual property agreements outside the WTO.

The TRIPS Agreement has an additional important principle: intellectual property protection should contribute to technical innovation and the transfer of technology. Both producers and users should benefit, and economic and social welfare should be enhanced, the agreement says.

How to protect intellectual property: common ground-rules

The second part of the TRIPS agreement looks at different kinds of intellectual property rights and how to protect them. The purpose is to ensure that adequate standards of protection exist in all member countries. Here the starting point is the obligations of the main international agreements of the World Intellectual Property Organization (WIPO) that already existed before the WTO was created:

the Paris Convention for the Protection of Industrial Property (patents, industrial designs, etc)
the Berne Convention for the Protection of Literary and Artistic Works (copyright).

Some areas are not covered by these conventions. In some cases, the standards of protection prescribed were thought inadequate.

So the TRIPS agreement adds a significant number of new or higher standards.

Copyright

The TRIPS agreement ensures that computer programs will be protected as literary works under the Berne Convention and outlines how databases should be protected.

It also expands international copyright rules to cover rental rights. Authors of computer programs and producers of sound recordings must have the right to prohibit the commercial rental of their works to the public. A similar exclusive right applies to films where commercial rental has led to widespread copying, affecting copyright-owners' potential earnings from their films.

The agreement says performers must also have the right to prevent unauthorized recording, reproduction and broadcast of live performances (bootlegging) for no less than 50 years. Producers of sound recordings must have the right to prevent the unauthorized reproduction of recordings for a period of 50 years.

Trademarks

The agreement defines what types of signs must be eligible for protection as trademarks, and what the minimum rights conferred on their owners must be. It says that service marks must be protected in the same way as trademarks used for goods. Marks that have become well-known in a particular country enjoy additional protection.

Geographical indications

A place name is sometimes used to identify a product. This "geographical indication" does not only say where the product was made. More importantly, it identifies the product's special characteristics, which are the result of the product's origins.

Well-known examples include "Champagne", "Scotch", "Tequila", and "Roquefort" cheese. Wine and spirits makers are particularly concerned about the use of place-names to identify products, and the TRIPS Agreement contains special provisions for these products. But the issue is also important for other types of goods.

Using the place name when the product was made elsewhere or when it does not have the usual characteristics can mislead consumers, and it can lead to unfair competition. The TRIPS Agreement says countries have to prevent this misuse of place names.

For wines and spirits, the agreement provides higher levels of protection, i.e. even where there is no danger of the public being misled.

Some exceptions are allowed, for example if the name is already protected as a trademark or if it has become a generic term. For example, "cheddar" now refers to a particular type of cheese not necessarily made in Cheddar, in the UK. But any country wanting to make an exception for these reasons must be willing to negotiate with the country which wants to protect the geographical indication in question.

The agreement provides for further negotiations in the WTO to establish a multilateral system of notification and registration of geographical indications for wines. These are now part of the Doha Development Agenda and they include spirits. Also debated in the WTO is whether to negotiate extending this higher level of protection beyond wines and spirits.

Industrial designs

Under the TRIPS Agreement, industrial designs must be protected for at least 10 years. Owners of protected designs must be able to prevent the manufacture, sale or importation of articles bearing or embodying a design which is a copy of the protected design.

Types of intellectual property

The areas covered by the TRIPS Agreem

ent
- Copyright and related rights
- Trademarks, including service marks
- Geographical indications
- Industrial designs
- Patents
- Layout-designs (topographies) of integrat

ed circuits

Undisclosed information, including trade secrets

Patents

The agreement says patent protection must be available for inventions for at least 20 years. Patent protection must be available for both products and processes, in almost all fields of technology. Governments can refuse to issue a patent for an invention if its commercial exploitation is prohibited for reasons of public order or morality. They can also exclude diagnostic, therapeutic and surgical methods, plants and animals (other than microorganisms), and biological processes for the production of plants or animals (other than microbiological processes).

Plant varieties, however, must be protectable by patents or by a special system (such as the breeder's rights provided in the conventions of UPOV — the International Union for the Protection of New Varieties of Plants).

The agreement describes the minimum rights that a patent owner must enjoy. But it also allows certain exceptions. A patent owner could abuse his rights, for example by failing to supply the product on the market. To deal with that possibility, the agreement says governments can issue "compulsory licences", allowing a competitor to produce the product or use the process under licence. But this can only be done under certain conditions aimed at safeguarding the legitimate interests of the patent-holder.

If a patent is issued for a production process, then the rights must extend to the product directly obtained from the process. Under certain conditions alleged infringers may be ordered by a court to prove that they have not used the patented process.

An issue that has arisen recently is how to ensure patent protection for pharmaceutical products does not prevent people in poor countries from having access to medicines — while at the same time maintaining the patent system's role in providing incentives for research and development into new medicines. Flexibilities such as compulsory licensing are written into the TRIPS Agreement, but some governments were unsure of how these would be interpreted, and how far their right to use them would be respected.

A large part of this was settled when WTO ministers issued a special declaration at the Doha Ministerial Conference in November 2001. They agreed that the TRIPS Agreement does not and should not prevent members from taking measures to protect public health. They underscored countries' ability to use the flexibilities that are built into the TRIPS Agreement. And they agreed to extend exemptions on pharmaceutical patent protection for least-developed countries until 2016. On one remaining question, they assigned further work to the TRIPS Council — to sort out how to provide extra flexibility, so that countries unable to produce pharmaceuticals domestically can import patented drugs made under compulsory licensing. A waiver providing this flexibility was agreed on 30 August 2003.

Integrated circuits layout designs

The basis for protecting integrated circuit designs ("topographies") in the TRIPS agreement is the Washington Treaty on Intellectual Property in Respect of Integrated Circuits, which comes under the <u>World Intellectual Property Organization</u>. This was adopted in 1989 but has not yet entered into force. The TRIPS agreement adds a number of provisions: for example, protection must be available for at least 10 years.

Undisclosed information and trade secrets

Trade secrets and other types of "undisclosed information" which have commercial value must be protected against breach of confidence and other acts contrary to honest commercial practices. But reasonable steps must have been taken to keep the information secret. Test data submitted to governments in order to obtain marketing approval for new pharmaceutical or agricultural chemicals must also be protected against unfair commercial use.

Curbing anti-competitive licensing contracts

The owner of a copyright, patent or other form of intellectual property right can issue a licence for someone else to produce or copy the protected trademark, work, invention, design, etc. The agreement recognizes that the terms of a licensing contract could restrict competition or impede technology transfer. It says that under certain conditions, governments have the right to take action to prevent anti-competitive licensing that abuses intellectual property rights. It also says governments must be prepared to consult each other on controlling anti-competitive licensing.

Enforcement: tough but fair

Having intellectual property laws is not enough. They have to be enforced. This is covered in Part 3 of TRIPS. The agreement says governments have to ensure that intellectual property rights can be enforced under their laws, and that the penalties for infringement are tough enough to deter further violations. The procedures must be fair and equitable, and not unnecessarily complicated or costly. They should not entail unreasonable time-limits or unwarranted delays. People involved should be able to ask a court to review an administrative decision or to appeal a lower court's ruling.

The agreement describes in some detail how enforcement should be handled, including rules for obtaining evidence, provisional measures, injunctions, damages and other penalties. It says courts should have the right, under certain conditions, to order the disposal or destruction of pirated or counterfeit goods. Wilful trademark counterfeiting or copyright piracy on a commercial scale should be criminal offences. Governments should make sure that intellectual property rights owners can receive the assistance of customs authorities to prevent imports of counterfeit and pirated goods.

Technology transfer

Developing countries in particular, see technology transfer as part of the bargain in which they have agreed to protect intellectual property rights. The TRIPS Agreement includes a number of provisions on this. For example, it requires developed countries' governments to provide incentives for their companies to transfer technology to least-developed countries.

Transition arrangements: 1, 5 or 11 years or more

When the WTO agreements took effect on 1 January 1995, developed countries were given one year to ensure that their laws and practices conform with the TRIPS agreement. Developing countries and (under certain conditions) transition economies were given five years, until 2000. Least-developed countries had 11 years, until 2006 — now extended to 2013 in general, and to 2016 for pharmaceutical patents and undisclosed information.

If a developing country did not provide product patent protection in a particular area of technology when the TRIPS Agreement became applicable to it (1 January 2000), it had up to five additional years to introduce the protection. But for pharmaceutical and agricultural chemical products, the country had to accept the filing of patent applications from the beginning of the transitional period (i.e. 1 January 1995), though the patent did not need to be granted until the end of this period. If the government allowed the relevant pharmaceutical or agricultural chemical to be marketed during the transition period, it had to — subject to certain conditions — provide an exclusive marketing right for the product for five years, or until a product patent was granted, whichever was shorter.

Subject to certain exceptions, the general rule is that obligations in the agreement apply to intellectual property rights that existed at the end of a country's transition period as well as to new ones.

If a company exports a product at a price lower than the price it normally charges on its own home market, it is said to be "dumping" the product. Is this unfair competition? Opinions differ, but many governments take action against dumping in order to defend their domestic industries. The WTO agreement does not pass judgement. Its focus is on how governments can or cannot react to dumping — it disciplines anti-dumping actions, and it is often called the **"Anti-Dumping Agreement"**. (This focus only on the reaction to dumping contrasts with the approach of the Subsidies and Countervailing Measures Agreement.)

Chapter – 12

Anti Dumping And Subsidies and Counterveiling measures

The legal definitions are more precise, but broadly speaking the WTO agreement allows governments to act against dumping where there is genuine ("material") injury to the competing domestic industry. In order to do that the government has to be able to show that dumping is taking place, calculate the extent of dumping (how much lower the export price is compared to the exporter's home market price), and show that the dumping is causing injury or threatening to do so.

GATT (Article 6) allows countries to take action against dumping. The Anti-Dumping Agreement clarifies and expands Article 6, and the two operate together. They allow countries to act in a way that would normally break the GATT principles of <u>binding</u> a tariff and <u>not discriminating</u> between trading partners — typically anti-dumping action means charging extra import duty on the particular product from the particular exporting country in order to bring its price closer to the "normal value" or to remove the injury to domestic industry in the importing country.

There are many different ways of calculating whether a particular product is being dumped heavily or only lightly. The agreement narrows down the range of possible options. It provides three methods to calculate a product's "normal value". The main one is based on the price in the exporter's domestic market. When this cannot be used, two alternatives are available — the price charged by the exporter in another country, or a calculation based on the combination of the exporter's production costs, other expenses and normal profit margins. And the agreement also specifies how a fair comparison can be made between the export price and what would be a normal price.

Calculating the extent of dumping on a product is not enough. Anti-dumping measures can only be applied if the dumping is hurting the industry in the importing country. Therefore, a detailed investigation has to be conducted according to specified rules first. The investigation must evaluate all relevant economic factors that have a bearing on the state of the industry in question. If the investigation shows dumping is taking place and domestic industry is being hurt, the exporting company can undertake to raise its price to an agreed level in order to avoid anti-dumping import duty.

Detailed procedures are set out on how anti-dumping cases are to be initiated, how the investigations are to be conducted, and the conditions for ensuring that all interested parties are given an opportunity to present evidence. Anti-dumping measures must expire five years after the date of imposition, unless an investigation shows that ending the measure would lead to injury.

Anti-dumping investigations are to end immediately in cases where the authorities determine that the margin of dumping is insignificantly small (defined as less than 2% of the export price of the product). Other conditions are also set. For example, the investigations also have to end if the volume of dumped imports is negligible (i.e. if the volume from one country is less than 3% of total imports of that product — although investigations can proceed if several countries, each supplying less than 3% of the imports, together account for 7% or more of total imports).

The agreement says member countries must inform the Committee on Anti-Dumping Practices about all preliminary and final anti-dumping actions, promptly and in detail. They must also report on all investigations twice a year. When differences arise, members are encouraged to consult each other. They can also use the WTO's dispute settlement procedure.

>

> See also

What is this agreement called?

Agreement on the implementation of Article VI [i.e 6] of the General Agreement on Tariffs and Trade 1994

Subsidies and countervailing measures

This agreement does two things: it disciplines the use of subsidies, and it regulates the actions countries can take to counter the effects of subsidies. It says a country can use the WTO's to seek the withdrawal of the subsidy or the removal of its adverse effects. Or the country can launch its own investigation and ultimately charge extra duty (known as "countervailing duty") on subsidized imports that are found to be hurting domestic producers.

The agreement contains a definition of subsidy. It also introduces the concept of a "specific" subsidy — i.e. a subsidy available only to an enterprise, industry, group of enterprises, or group of industries in the country (or state, etc) that gives the subsidy. The disciplines set out in the agreement only apply to specific subsidies. They can be domestic or export subsidies.

The agreement defines two categories of subsidies: prohibited and actionable. It originally contained a third category: non-actionable subsidies. This category existed for five years, ending on 31 December 1999, and was not extended. The agreement applies to agricultural goods as well as industrial products, except when the subsidies are exempt under the Agriculture Agreement's "peace clause", due to expire at the end of 2003.

Prohibited subsidies: subsidies that require recipients to meet certain export targets, or to use domestic goods instead of imported goods. They are prohibited because they are specifically designed to distort international trade, and are therefore likely to hurt other countries' trade. They can be challenged in the WTO dispute settlement procedure where they are handled under an accelerated timetable. If the dispute settlement procedure confirms that the subsidy is prohibited, it must be withdrawn immediately. Otherwise, the complaining country can take counter measures. If domestic producers are hurt by imports of subsidized products, countervailing duty can be imposed.

Actionable subsidies: in this category the

complaining country has to show that the subsidy has an adverse effect on its interests. Otherwise the subsidy is permitted. The agreement defines three types of damage they can cause. One country's subsidies can hurt a domestic industry in an importing country. They can hurt rival exporters from another country when the two compete in third markets. And domestic subsidies in one country can hurt exporters trying to compete in the subsidizing country's domestic market. If the Dispute Settlement Body rules that the subsidy does have an adverse effect, the subsidy must be withdrawn or its adverse effect must be removed. Again, if domestic producers are hurt by imports of subsidized products, countervailing duty can be imposed.

Some of the disciplines are similar to those of the Anti-Dumping Agreement. Countervailing duty (the parallel of anti-dumping duty) can only be charged after the importing country has conducted a detailed investigation similar to that required for anti-dumping action. There are detailed rules for deciding whether a product is being subsidized (not always an easy calculation), criteria for determining whether imports of subsidized products are hurting ("causing injury to") domestic industry, procedures for initiating and conducting investigations, and rules on the implementation and duration (normally five years) of countervailing measures. The subsidized exporter can also agree to raise its export prices as an alternative to its exports being charged countervailing duty.

Subsidies may play an important role in developing countries and in the transformation of centrally-planned economies to market economies. Least-developed countries and developing countries with less than $1,000 per capita GNP are exempted from disciplines on prohibited export subsidies. Other developing countries are given until 2003 to get rid of their export subsidies. Least-developed countries must eliminate import-substitution subsidies (i.e. subsidies designed to help domestic production and avoid importing) by 2003 — for other developing countries the deadline was 2000. Developing countries also receive preferential treatment if their exports are subject to countervailing duty investigations. For transition economies, prohibited subsidies had to be phased out by 2002.

>

> See also

Safeguards: emergency protection from imports

A WTO member may restrict imports of a product temporarily (take "safeguard" actions) if its domestic industry is injured or threatened with injury caused by a surge in imports. Here, the injury has to be serious. Safeguard measures were always available under GATT (Article 19). However, they were infrequently used, some governments preferring to protect their domestic industries through "grey area" measures — using bilateral negotiations outside GATT's auspices, they persuaded exporting countries to restrain exports "voluntarily" or to agree to other means of sharing markets. Agreements of this kind were reached for a wide range of products: automobiles, steel, and semiconductors, for example.

The WTO agreement broke new ground. It

prohibits "grey-area" measures, and it sets time limits (a "sunset clause") on all safeguard actions. The agreement says members must not seek, take or maintain any voluntary export restraints, orderly marketing arrangements or any other similar measures on the export or the import side. The bilateral measures that were not modified to conform with the agreement were phased out at the end of 1998. Countries were allowed to keep one of these measures an extra year (until the end of 1999), but only the European Union — for restrictions on imports of cars from Japan — made use of this provision.

An import "surge" justifying safeguard action can be a real increase in imports (an *absolute increase*); or it can be an increase in the imports' share of a shrinking market, even if the import quantity has not increased (*relative increase*).

Industries or companies may request safeguard action by their government. The WTO agreement sets out requirements for safeguard investigations by national authorities. The emphasis is on transparency and on following established rules and practices — avoiding arbitrary methods. The authorities conducting investigations have to announce publicly when hearings are to take place and provide other appropriate means for interested parties to present evidence. The evidence must include arguments on whether a measure is in the public interest.

The agreement sets out criteria for assessing whether "serious injury" is being caused or threatened, and the factors which must be considered in determining the impact of imports on the domestic industry. When imposed, a safeguard measure should be applied only to the extent necessary to prevent or remedy serious injury and to help the industry concerned to adjust. Where quantitative restrictions (quotas) are imposed, they normally should not reduce the quantities of imports below the annual average for the last three representative years for which statistics are available, unless clear justification is given that a different level is necessary to prevent or remedy serious injury.

In principle, safeguard measures cannot be targeted at imports from a particular country.

However, the agreement does describe how quotas can be allocated among supplying countries, including in the exceptional circumstance where imports from certain countries have increased disproportionately quickly. A safeguard measure should not last more than four years, although this can be extended up to eight years, subject to a determination by competent national authorities that the measure is needed and that there is evidence the industry is adjusting. Measures imposed for more than a year must be progressively liberalized.

When a country restricts imports in order to safeguard its domestic producers, in principle it must give something in return. The agreement says the exporting country (or exporting countries) can seek compensation through consultations. If no agreement is reached the exporting country can retaliate by taking equivalent action — for instance, it can raise tariffs on exports from the country that is enforcing the safeguard measure. In some circumstances, the exporting country has to wait for three years after the safeguard measure was introduced before it can retaliate in this way — i.e. if the measure conforms with the provisions of the agreement and if it is taken as a result of an increase in the quantity of imports from the exporting country.

To some extent developing countries' exports are shielded from safeguard actions. An importing country can only apply a safeguard measure to a product from a developing country if the developing country is supplying more than 3% of the imports of that product, or if developing country members with less than 3% import share collectively account for more than 9% of total imports of the product concerned.

The WTO's Safeguards Committee oversees the operation of the agreement and is responsible for the surveillance of members' commitments. Governments have to report each phase of a safeguard investigation and related decision-making, and the committee reviews these reports.

Although less widely used now than in the past, import licensing systems are subject to disciplines in the WTO. The **Agreement on Import Licensing Procedures** says import licensing should be simple, transparent and predictable. For example, the agreement requires governments to publish sufficient information for traders to know how and why the licences are granted. It also describes how countries should notify the WTO when they introduce new import licensing procedures or change existing procedures. The agreement offers guidance on how governments should assess applications for licences.

Some licences are issued automatically if certain conditions are met. The agreement sets criteria for automatic licensing so that the procedures used do not restrict trade.

Other licences are not issued automatically. Here, the agreement tries to minimize the importers' burden in applying for licences, so that the administrative work does not in itself restrict or distort imports. The agreement says the agencies handling licensing should not normally take more than 30 days to deal with an application — 60 days when all applications are considered at the same time.

>

Rules for the valuation of goods at customs

For importers, the process of estimating the value of a product at customs presents problems that can be just as serious as the actual duty rate charged. The WTO agreement on customs valuation aims for a fair, uniform and neutral system for the valuation of goods for customs purposes — a system that conforms to commercial realities, and which outlaws the use of arbitrary or fictitious customs values. The agreement provides a set of valuation rules, expanding and giving greater precision to the provisions on customs valuation in the original GATT.

A related Uruguay Round ministerial decision gives customs administrations the right to request further information in cases where they have reason to doubt the accuracy of the declared value of imported goods. If the administration maintains a reasonable doubt, despite any additional information, it may be deemed that the customs value of the imported goods cannot be determined on the basis of the declared value.

Preshipment inspection: a further check on imports

Preshipment inspection is the practice of employing specialized private companies (or "independent entities") to check shipment details — essentially price, quantity and quality — of goods ordered overseas. Used by governments of developing countries, the purpose is to safeguard national financial interests (preventing capital flight, commercial fraud, and customs duty evasion, for instance) and to compensate for inadequacies in administrative infrastructures.

The Preshipment Inspection Agreement recognizes that GATT principles and obligations apply to the activities of preshipment inspection agencies mandated by governments. The obligations placed on governments which use preshipment inspections include non-discrimination, transparency, protection of confidential business information, avoiding unreasonable delay, the use of specific guidelines for conducting price verification and avoiding conflicts of interest by the inspection agencies. The obligations of exporting members towards countries using preshipment inspection include non-discrimination in the application of domestic laws and regulations, prompt publication of those laws and regulations and the provision of technical assistance where requested.

The agreement establishes an independent review procedure. This is administered jointly by the International Federation of Inspection Agencies (IFIA), representing inspection agencies, and the International Chamber of Commerce (ICC), representing exporters. Its purpose is to resolve disputes between an exporter and an inspection agency.

Rules of origin: made in ... where?

"Rules of origin" are the criteria used to define

where a product was made. They are an essential part of trade rules because a number of policies discriminate between exporting countries: quotas, preferential tariffs, anti-dumping actions, countervailing duty (charged to counter export subsidies), and more. Rules of origin are also used to compile trade statistics, and for "made in ..." labels that are attached to products. This is complicated by globalization and the way a product can be processed in several countries before it is ready for the market.

The **Rules of Origin Agreement** requires WTO members to ensure that their rules of origin are transparent; that they do not have restricting, distorting or disruptive effects on international trade; that they are administered in a consistent, uniform, impartial and reasonable manner; and that they are based on a positive standard (in other words, they should state what *does confer origin rather than what does not*).

For the longer term, the agreement aims for common ("harmonized") rules of origin among all WTO members, except in some kinds of preferential trade — for example, countries setting up a free trade area are allowed to use different rules of origin for products traded under their free trade agreement. The agreement establishes a harmonization work programme, based upon a set of principles, including making rules of origin objective, understandable and predictable. The work was due to end in July 1998, but several deadlines have been missed. It is being conducted by a Committee on Rules of Origin in the WTO and a Technical Committee under the auspices of the World Customs Organization in Brussels. The outcome will be a single set of rules of origin to be applied under non-preferential trading conditions by all WTO members in all circumstances.

An annex to the agreement sets out a "common declaration" dealing with the operation of rules of origin on goods which qualify for preferential treatment.

>

Investment measures: reducing trade distortions

The **Trade-Related Investment Measures (TRIMs) Agreement** applies only to measures that affect trade in goods. It recognizes that certain measures can restrict and distort trade, and states that no member shall apply any measure that discriminates against foreigners or foreign products (i.e. violates "national treatment" principles in GATT). It also outlaws investment measures that lead to restrictions in quantities (violating another principle in GATT). An illustrative list of TRIMs agreed to be inconsistent with these GATT articles is appended to the agreement. The list includes measures which require particular levels of local procurement by an enterprise ("local content requirements"). It also discourages measures which limit a company's imports or set targets for the company to export ("trade balancing requirements").

Under the agreement, countries must inform fellow-members through the WTO of all investment measures that do not conform with the agreement. Developed countries had to eliminate these in two years (by the end of 1996); developing countries had five years (to the end of 1999); and least-developed countries seven. In July 2001, the Goods Council agreed to extend this transition period for a number of requesting developing countries.

The agreement establishes a Committee on TRIMs to monitor the implementation of these commitments. The agreement also says that WTO members should consider, by 1 January 2000, whether there should also be provisions on investment policy and competition policy. This discussion is now part of the Doha Development Agenda.

The <u>Agreement on Trade in Civil Aircraft</u> entered into force on 1 January 1980. It now has 30 signatories. The agreement eliminates import duties on all aircraft, other than military aircraft, as well as on all other products covered by the agreement — civil aircraft engines and their parts and components, all components and sub-assemblies of civil aircraft, and flight simulators and their parts and components. It contains disciplines on government-directed procurement of civil aircraft and inducements to purchase, as well as on government financial support for the civil aircraft sector.

>

Government procurement: opening up for competition

In most countries the government, and the agencies it controls, are together the biggest purchasers of goods of all kinds, ranging from basic commodities to high-technology equipment. At the same time, the political pressure to favour domestic suppliers over their foreign competitors can be very strong.

An [Agreement on Government Procurement]() was first negotiated during the Tokyo Round and entered into force on 1 January 1981. Its purpose is to open up as much of this business as possible to international competition. It is designed to make laws, regulations, procedures and practices regarding government procurement more transparent and to ensure they do not protect domestic products or suppliers, or discriminate against foreign products or suppliers.

The agreement has 28 members. It has two elements — general rules and obligations, and schedules of national entities in each member country whose procurement is subject to the agreement. A large part of the general rules and obligations concern tendering procedures.

The present agreement and commitments were negotiated in the Uruguay Round. These negotiations achieved a 10-fold expansion of coverage, extending international competition to include national and local government entities whose collective purchases are worth several hundred billion dollars each year. The new agreement also extends coverage to services (including construction services), procurement at the sub-central level (for example, states, provinces, departments and prefectures), and procurement by public utilities. The new agreement took effect on 1 January 1996.

It also reinforces rules guaranteeing fair and non-discriminatory conditions of international competition. For example, governments will be required to put in place domestic procedures by which aggrieved private bidders can challenge procurement decisions and obtain redress in the event such decisions were made inconsistently with the rules of the agreement.

The agreement applies to contracts worth more than specified threshold values. For central government purchases of goods and services, the threshold is SDR 130,000 (some $185,000 in June 2003). For purchases of goods and services by sub-central government entities the threshold varies but is generally in the region of SDR 200,000. For utilities, thresholds for goods and services is generally in the area of SDR 400,000 and for construction contracts, in general the threshold value is SDR 5,000,000.

>

Dairy and bovine meat agreements: ended in 1997

The <u>International Dairy Agreement</u> and <u>International Bovine Meat Agreement</u> were scrapped at the end of 1997. Countries that had signed the agreements decided that the sectors were better handled under the Agriculture and Sanitary and Phytosanitary agreements. Some aspects of their work had been handicapped by the small number of signatories. For example, some major exporters of dairy products did not sign the Dairy Agreement, and the attempt to cooperate on minimum prices therefore failed — minimum pricing was suspended in 1995.

The importance countries attach to the process is reflected in the seniority of the Trade Policy Review Body — it is the WTO General Council in another guise.

The objectives are:

to increase the transparency and understanding of countries' trade policies and practices, through regular monitoring

to improve the quality of public and intergovernmental debate on the issues to enable a multilateral assessment of the effects of policies on the world trading system.

The reviews focus on members' own trade policies and practices. But they also take into account the countries' wider economic and developmental needs, their policies and objectives, and the external economic environment that they face. These "peer reviews" by other WTO members encourage governments to follow more closely the WTO rules and disciplines and to fulfil their commitments. In practice the reviews have two broad results: they enable outsiders to understand a country's policies and circumstances, and they provide feedback to the reviewed country on its performance in the system.

Over a period of time, all WTO members are to come under scrutiny. The frequency of the reviews depends on the country's size:

The four biggest traders — the European Union, the United States, Japan and China (the "Quad") — are examined approximately once every two years.

The next 16 countries (in terms of their share of world trade) are reviewed every four years.

The remaining countries are reviewed every six years, with the possibility of a longer interim period for the least-developed countries.

For each review, two documents are prepared: a policy statement by the government under review, and a detailed report written independently by the WTO Secretariat. These two reports, together with the proceedings of the Trade Policy Review Body's meetings are published shortly afterwards.

Chapter – 13
Trade Policy Review Mechanisms

Disputes in the WTO are essentially about broken promises. WTO members have agreed that if they believe fellow-members are violating trade rules, they will use the multilateral system of settling disputes instead of taking action unilaterally. That means abiding by the agreed procedures, and respecting judgements.

A dispute arises when one country adopts a trade policy measure or takes some action that one or more fellow-WTO members considers to be breaking the WTO agreements, or to be a failure to live up to obligations. A third group of countries can declare that they have an interest in the case and enjoy some rights.

A procedure for settling disputes existed under the old GATT, but it had no fixed timetables, rulings were easier to block, and many cases dragged on for a long time inconclusively. The Uruguay Round agreement introduced a more structured process with more clearly defined stages in the procedure. It introduced greater discipline for the length of time a case should take to be settled, with flexible deadlines set in various stages of the procedure. The agreement emphasizes that prompt settlement is essential if the WTO is to function effectively. It sets out in considerable detail the procedures and the timetable to be followed in resolving disputes. If a case runs its full course to a first ruling, it should not normally take more than about one year — 15 months if the case is appealed. The agreed time limits are flexible, and if the case is considered urgent (e.g. if perishable goods are involved), it is accelerated as much as possible.

The Uruguay Round agreement also made it impossible for the country losing a case to block the adoption of the ruling. Under the previous

GATT procedure, rulings could only be adopted by consensus, meaning that a single objection could block the ruling. Now, rulings are automatically adopted unless there is a consensus to reject a ruling — any country wanting to block a ruling has to persuade all other WTO members (including its adversary in the case) to share its view.

Although much of the procedure does resemble a court or tribunal, the preferred solution is for the countries concerned to discuss their problems and settle the dispute by themselves. The first stage is therefore consultations between the governments concerned, and even when the case has progressed to other stages, consultation and mediation are still always possible.

How long to settle a dispute?

These approximate

periods for each stage of a dispute settlement procedure are target figures — the agreement is flexible. In addition, the countries can settle their dispute themsel ves at any stage. Totals are also approximate.

60 days	Consultations, mediation, etc
45 days	Panel set up and panellists appointed
6 months	Final panel report to parties
3	Final

weeks	panel report to WTO members
60 days	Dispute Settlement Body adopts report (if no appeal)
Total = 1 year	**(without appeal)**
60-90 days	Appeals report
30 days	Dispute Settlement Body adopts

appeals report

Total = (with 1y 3m appeal)

What is this agreement called?
Understanding on Rules and Procedures Governing the Settlement of Disputes

More cases can be good news

If the courts find themselves handling an increasing number

of criminal cases, does that mean law and order is breaking down? Not necessarily. Sometimes it means that people have more faith in the courts and the rule of law. They are turning to the courts instead of taking the law into their own hands.

For the most part, that is what is happening in the WTO. No one likes to see countries quarrel. But if there are going to be trade disputes anyway, it is healthier that the cases are handled according to internationally agreed rules. There are strong grounds for arguing that the increasing number of disputes is simply the result of expanding world trade and the stricter rules negotiated in the Uruguay Round; and that the fact that more are coming to the WTO reflects a growing faith in the system.

How are disputes settled?

Settling disputes is the responsibility of the Dispute Settlement Body (the General Council in another guise), which consists of all WTO members. The Dispute Settlement Body has the sole authority to establish "panels" of experts to consider the case, and to accept or reject the panels' findings or the results of an appeal. It monitors the implementation of the rulings and recommendations, and has the power to authorize retaliation when a country does not comply with a ruling.

First stage: consultation (up to **60 days**). Before taking any other actions the countries in dispute have to talk to each other to see if they can settle their differences by themselves. If that fails, they can also ask the WTO director-general to mediate or try to help in any other way.

Second stage: the panel (up to **45 days** for a panel to be appointed, plus 6 months for the panel to conclude). If consultations fail, the complaining country can ask for a panel to be appointed. The country "in the dock" can block the creation of a panel once, but when the Dispute Settlement Body meets for a second time, the appointment can no longer be blocked (unless there is a consensus against appointing the panel).

Officially, the panel is helping the Dispute Settlement Body make rulings or recommendations. But because the panel's report can only be rejected by consensus in the Dispute Settlement Body, its conclusions are difficult to overturn. The panel's findings have to be based on the agreements cited.

The panel's final report should normally be given to the parties to the dispute within six months. In cases of urgency, including those concerning perishable goods, the deadline is shortened to three months.

The agreement describes in some detail how the panels are to work. The main stages are:

Before the first hearing: each side in the dispute presents its case in writing to the panel.

First hearing: the case for the complaining country and defence: the complaining country (or countries), the responding country, and those that have announced they have an interest in the dispute, make their case at the panel's first hearing.

Rebuttals: the countries involved submit written rebuttals and present oral arguments at the panel's second meeting.

Experts: if one side raises scientific or other technical matters, the panel may consult experts or appoint an expert review group to prepare an advisory report.

First draft: the panel submits the descriptive (factual and argument) sections of its report to the two sides, giving them two weeks to comment. This report does not include findings and conclusions.

Interim report: The panel then submits an interim report, including its findings and conclusions, to the two sides, giving them one week to ask for a review.

Review: The period of review must not exceed two weeks. During that time, the panel may hold additional meetings with the two sides.

Final report: A final report is submitted to the two sides and three weeks later, it is circulated to all WTO members. If the panel decides that the disputed trade measure does break a WTO agreement or an obligation, it recommends that the measure be made to conform with WTO rules. The panel may suggest how this could be done.

The report becomes a ruling: The report becomes the Dispute Settlement Body's ruling or recommendation within 60 days unless a consensus rejects it. Both sides can appeal the report (and in some cases both sides do).

Panels

Panels are like tribunals. But unlike in a normal tribunal, the panellists are usually chosen in consultation with the countries in dispute. Only if the two sides cannot agree does the WTO director-general appoint them.

Panels consist of three (possibly five)

experts from different countries who examine the evidence and decide who is right and who is wrong. The panel's report is passed to the Dispute Settlement

Body, which can only reject the report by consensus.

Panelists for each case may be chosen from an of well-qualified candidates nominated by WTO

Members, although others may be considered as well, including those who have formerly served as panelist. Panelists serve in their individual capaciti es. They cannot receive instructions from any government. The indicative list is maintained by the Secretariat and periodically revised according to any modifications or additions submitted by Members.

Appeals

Either side can appeal a panel's ruling. Sometimes both sides do so. Appeals have to be based on points of law such as legal interpretation — they cannot reexamine existing evidence or examine new issues.

Each appeal is heard by three members of a permanent seven-member Appellate Body set up by the Dispute Settlement Body and broadly representing the range of WTO membership. Members of the Appellate Body have four-year terms. They have to be individuals with recognized standing in the field of law and international trade, not affiliated with any government.

The appeal can uphold, modify or reverse the panel's legal findings and conclusions. Normally appeals should not last more than 60 days, with an absolute maximum of 90 days.

The Dispute Settlement Body has to accept or reject the appeals report within 30 days — and rejection is only possible by consensus.

The case has been decided: what next?

Go directly to jail. Do not pass Go, do not collect … . Well, not exactly. But the sentiments apply. If a country has done something wrong, it should swiftly correct its fault. And if it continues to break an agreement, it should offer compensation or suffer a suitable penalty that has some bite.

Even once the case has been decided, there is more to do before trade sanctions (the conventional form of penalty) are imposed. The priority at this stage is for the losing "defendant" to bring its policy into line with the ruling or recommendations. The dispute settlement agreement stresses that "prompt compliance with recommendations or rulings of the DSB [Dispute Settlement Body] is essential in order to ensure effective resolution of disputes to the benefit of all Members".

If the country that is the target of the complaint loses, it must follow the recommendations of the panel report or the appeals report. It must state its intention to do so at a Dispute Settlement Body meeting held within 30 days of the report's adoption. If complying with the recommendation immediately proves impractical, the member will be given a "reasonable period of time" to do so. If it fails to act within this period, it has to enter into negotiations with the complaining country (or countries) in order to determine mutually-acceptable compensation — for instance, tariff reductions in areas of particular interest to the complaining side.

If after 20 days, no satisfactory compensation is agreed, the complaining side may ask the Dispute Settlement Body for permission to impose limited trade sanctions ("suspend concessions or obligations") against the other side. The Dispute Settlement Body must grant this authorization within 30 days of the expiry of the "reasonable period of time" unless there is a consensus against the request.

In principle, the sanctions should be imposed in the same sector as the dispute. If this is not practical or if it would not be effective, the sanctions can be imposed in a different sector of the same agreement. In turn, if this is not effective or practicable and if the circumstances are serious enough, the action can be taken under another agreement. The objective is to minimize the chances of actions spilling over into unrelated sectors while at the same time allowing the actions to be effective.

In any case, the Dispute Settlement Body monitors how adopted rulings are implemented. Any outstanding case remains on its agenda until the issue is resolved.

The United States and Venezuela then took six and a half months to agree on what the United States should do. The agreed period for implementing the solution was 15 months from the date the appeal was concluded (20 May 1996 to 20 August 1997).

The case arose because the United States applied stricter rules on the chemical characteristics of imported gasoline than it did for domestically-refined gasoline. Venezuela (and later Brazil) said this was unfair because US gasoline did not have to meet the same standards — it violated the "national treatment" principle and could not be justified under exceptions to normal WTO rules for health and environmental conservation measures. The dispute panel agreed with Venezuela and Brazil. The appeal report upheld the panel's conclusions (making some changes to the panel's legal interpretation). The United States agreed with Venezuela that it would amend its regulations within 15 months and on 26 August 1997 it reported to the Dispute

Settlement Body that a new regulation had been signed on 19 August.

Time (0 = start of case)	Target/actual period	Date	Action
-5 years		1990	US Clean Air Act amended
-4 months		September 1994	US restricts gasoline imports under Clean Air Act
0	*"60 days"*	23 January 1995	Venezuela complains to Dispute

			Settlement Body, asks for consultation with US
+1 month		24 February 1995	Consultations take place. Fail.
+2 months		25 March 1995	Venezuela asks Dispute Settlement Body for a panel
+2½ months	*"30 days"*	10 April 1995	Dispute Settlement

		Body agrees to appoint panel. US does not block. (Brazil starts complaint, requests consultation with US.)
+3 months	28 April 1995	Panel appointed. (31 May, panel assigne

			d to Brazilian complaint as well)
+6 months	9 months *(target is 6-9)*	10-12 July and 13-15 July 1995	Panel meets
+11 months		11 December 1995	Panel gives interim report to US, Venezuela and Brazil for comment
+1 year		29 January	Panel circulat

		1996	es final report to members
+1 year, 1 month		21 February 1996	US appeals
+1 year, 3 months	*"60 days"*	29 April 1996	Appellate Body submits report
+1 year, 4 months	*"30 days"*	20 May 1996	Dispute Settlement Body adopts panel and appeal reports
+1 year, 10½		3 December	US and Venezuela

months	1996	agree on what US should do (implementation period is 15 months from 20 May)
+1 year, 11½ months	9 January 1997	US makes first of monthly reports to Dispute Settlement Body on

			status of implementation
+2 years, 7 months		19-20 August 1997	US signs new regulation (19th). End of agreed implementation period (20th)

By July 2005, only one WTO member — Mongolia, — was not party to a regional trade agreement. The surge in these agreements has continued unabated since the early 1990s. By July 2005, a total of 330 had been notified to the WTO (and its predecessor, GATT). Of these: 206 were notified after the WTO was created in January 1995; 180 are currently in force; several others are believed to be operational although not yet notified.

One of the most frequently asked questions is whether these regional groups help or hinder the WTO's multilateral trading system. A committee is keeping an eye on developments.

Regional trading arrangements

They seem to be contraditory, but often regional trade agreements can actually support the WTO's multilateral trading system. Regional agreements have allowed groups of countries to negotiate rules and commitments that go beyond what was possible at the time multilaterally. In turn, some of these rules have paved the way for agreement in the WTO. Services, intellectual property, , investment and competition policies are all issues that were raised in regional negotiations and later developed into agreements or topics of discussion in the WTO.

The groupings that are important for the WTO

are those that abolish or reduce barriers on trade within the group. The WTO agreements recognize that regional arrangements and closer economic integration can benefit countries. It also recognizes that under some circumstances regional trading arrangements could hurt the trade interests of other countries. Normally, setting up a customs union or free trade area would violate the WTO's principle of equal treatment for all trading partners ("most-favoured-nation"). But **GATT's Article 24** allows regional trading arrangements to be set up as a special exception, provided certain strict criteria are met.

In particular, the arrangements should help trade flow more freely among the countries in the group without barriers being raised on trade with the outside world. In other words, regional integration should complement the multilateral trading system and not threaten it.

Article 24 says if a free trade area or customs union is created, duties and other trade barriers should be reduced or removed on substantially all sectors of trade in the group. Non-members should not find trade with the group any more restrictive than before the group was set up.

Similarly, Article 5 of the provides for economic integration agreements in services. Other provisions in the WTO agreements allow developing countries to enter into regional or global agreements that include the reduction or elimination of tariffs and non-tariff barriers on trade among themselves.

On 6 February 1996, the WTO General Council created the **Regional Trade Agreements Committee**. Its purpose is to examine regional groups and to assess whether they are consistent with WTO rules. The committee is also examining how regional arrangements might affect the multilateral trading system, and what the relationship between regional and multilateral arrangements might be.

The increased emphasis on environmental

policies is relatively recent in the 60-year history of the multilateral trading system. At the end of the Uruguay Round in 1994, trade ministers from participating countries decided to begin a comprehensive work programme on trade and environment in the WTO. They created the **Trade and Environment Committee**. This has brought environmental and sustainable development issues into the mainstream of WTO work. The 2001 Doha Ministerial Conference kicked off negotiations in some aspects of the subject.

> See also

The committee: broad-based responsibility

The committee has a broad-based responsibility covering all areas of the multilateral trading system — goods, services and intellectual property. Its duties are to study the relationship between trade and the environment, and to make recommendations about any changes that might be needed in the trade agreements.

The committee's work is based on two important principles:

The WTO is only competent to deal with trade. In other words, in environmental issues its only task is to study questions that arise when environmental policies have a significant impact on trade. The WTO is not an environmental agency. Its members do not want it to intervene in national or international environmental policies or to set environmental standards. Other agencies that specialize in environmental issues are better qualified to undertake those tasks.

If the committee does identify problems, its solutions must continue to uphold the .

More generally WTO members are convinced that an open, equitable and non-discriminatory multilateral trading system has a key contribution to make to national and international efforts to better protect and conserve environmental resources and promote sustainable development. This was recognized in the results of the 1992 UN Conference on Environment and Development in Rio (the "Earth Summit") and its 2002 successor, the World Summit on Sustainable Development in Johannesburg.

The committee's work programme focuses on 10 areas. Its agenda is driven by proposals from individual WTO members on issues of importance to them. The following sections outline some of the issues, and what the committee has concluded so far:

WTO and environmental agreements: how are they related?

How do the WTO trading system and "green" trade measures relate to each other? What is the relationship between the WTO agreements and various international environmental agreements and conventions?

There are about 200 international agreements (outside the WTO) dealing with various environmental issues currently in force. They are called multilateral environmental agreements (MEAs).

About 20 of these include provisions that can affect trade: for example they ban trade in certain products, or allow countries to restrict trade in certain circumstances. Among them are the Montreal Protocol for the protection of the ozone layer, the Basel Convention on the trade or transportation of hazardous waste across international borders, and the Convention on International Trade in Endangered Species (CITES).

Briefly, the WTO's committee says the basic of non-discrimination and transparency do not conflict with trade measures needed to protect the environment, including actions taken under the environmental agreements. It also notes that clauses in the agreements on goods, services and intellectual property allow governments to give priority to their domestic environmental policies.

The WTO's committee says the most effective way to deal with international environmental problems is through the environmental agreements. It says this approach complements the WTO's work in seeking internationally agreed solutions for trade problems. In other words, using the provisions of an international environmental agreement is better than one country trying on its own to change other countries' environmental policies (*see and studies*).

The committee notes that actions taken to protect the environment and having an impact on trade can play an important role in some environmental agreements, particularly when trade is a direct cause of the environmental problems. But it also points out that trade restrictions are not the only actions that can be taken, and they are not necessarily the most effective. Alternatives include: helping countries acquire environmentally-friendly technology, giving them financial assistance, providing training, etc.

The problem should not be exaggerated. So far, no action affecting trade and taken under an international environmental agreement has been challenged in the GATT-WTO system. There is also a widely held view that actions taken under an environmental agreement are unlikely to become a problem in the WTO if the countries concerned have signed the environmental agreement, although the question is not settled completely. The Trade and Environment Committee is more concerned about what happens when one country invokes an environmental agreement to take action against another country that has not signed the environmental agreement.

> See also

Disputes: where should they be handled?

Suppose a trade dispute arises because a country has taken action on trade (for example imposed a tax or restricted imports) under an environmental agreement outside the WTO and another country objects. Should the dispute be handled under the WTO or under the other agreement? The Trade and Environment Committee says that if a dispute arises over a trade action taken under an environmental agreement, and if both sides to the dispute have signed that agreement, then they should try to use the environmental agreement to settle the dispute. But if one side in the dispute has not signed the environment agreement, then the WTO would provide the only possible forum for settling the dispute. The preference for handling disputes under the environmental agreements does not mean environmental issues would be ignored in WTO disputes. The WTO agreements allow panels examining a dispute to seek expert advice on environmental issues.

A WTO dispute: The 'shrimp-turtle' case

This was a case brought by India, Malaysia, Pakistan and Thailand against the US. The appellate and panel reports were adopted on 6 November 1998. The official title is "United States — Import Prohibition of Certain Shrimp and Shrimp Products", the official WTO case numbers are 58 and 61.

What was it all about?

Seven species of sea turtles have been identified. They are distributed around the world in subtropical and tropical areas. They spend their lives at sea, where they migrate between their foraging and nesting grounds.

Sea turtles have been adversely affected by human activity, either directly (their meat, shells and eggs have been exploited), or indirectly (incidental capture in fisheries, destroyed habitats, polluted oceans).

In early 1997, India, Malaysia, Pakistan and Thailand brought a joint complaint against a ban imposed by the US on the importation of certain shrimp and shrimp products. The protection of sea turtles was at the heart of the ban.

The US Endangered Species Act of 1973 listed as endangered or threatened the five species of sea turtles that occur in US waters, and prohibited their "take" within the US, in its territorial sea and the high seas. ("Take" means harassment, hunting, capture, killing or attempting to do any of these.)

Under the act, the US required US shrimp trawlers to use "turtle excluder devices" (TEDs) in their nets when fishing in areas where there is a significant likelihood of encountering sea turtles.

Section 609 of US Public Law 101-102, enacted in 1989, dealt with imports. It said, among other things, that shrimp harvested with technology that may adversely affect certain sea turtles may not be imported into the US — unless the harvesting nation was certified to have a regulatory programme and an incidental take-rate comparable to that of the US, or that the particular fishing environment of the harvesting nation did not pose a threat to sea turtles.

In practice, countries that had any of the five species of sea turtles within their jurisdiction, and harvested shrimp with mechanical means, had to impose on their fishermen requirements comparable to those borne by US shrimpers if they wanted to be certified to export shrimp products to the US. Essentially this meant the use of TEDs at all times.

The ruling

In its report, the Appellate Body made clear that under WTO rules, countries have the right to take trade action to protect the environment (in particular, human, animal or plant life and health) and endangered species and exhaustible resources). The WTO does not have to "allow" them this right.

It also said measures to protect sea turtles would be legitimate under GATT Article 20 which deals with various exceptions to the WTO's trade rules, provided certain criteria such as non-discrimination were met.

The US lost the case, not because it sought to protect the environment but because it discriminated between WTO members. It provided countries in the western hemisphere — mainly in the Caribbean — technical and financial assistance and longer transition periods for their fishermen to start using turtle-excluder devices.

It did not give the same advantages, however, to the four Asian countries (India, Malaysia, Pakistan and Thailand) that filed the complaint with the WTO.

The ruling also said WTO panels may accept "amicus briefs" (friends-of-the-court submissions) from NGOs or other interested parties.

'What we have not decided ...'

This is part of what the Appellate Body said:

"185. In reaching these conclusions, we wish to underscore what we have not decided in this appeal. We have not decided that the protection and preservation of the environment is of no significance to the Members of the WTO. Clearly, it is. We have not decided that the sovereign nations that are Members of the WTO cannot adopt effective measures to protect endangered species, such as sea turtles. Clearly, they can and should. And we have not decided that sovereign states should not act together bilaterally, plurilaterally or multilaterally, either within the WTO or in other international fora, to protect endangered species or to otherwise protect the environment. Clearly, they should and do.

"186. What we have decided in this appeal is simply this: although the measure of the United States in dispute in this appeal serves an environmental objective that is recognized as legitimate under paragraph (g) of Article XX [i.e. 20] of the GATT 1994, this measure has been applied by the United States in a manner which constitutes arbitrary and unjustifiable discrimination between Members of the WTO, contrary to the requirements of the chapeau of Article XX. For all of the specific reasons outlined in this Report, this measure does not qualify for the exemption that Article XX of the GATT 1994 affords to measures which serve certain recognized, legitimate environmental purposes but which, at the same time, are not applied in a manner that constitutes a means of arbitrary or unjustifiable discrimination between countries where the same conditions prevail or a disguised restriction on international trade. As we emphasized in United States — Gasoline [adopted 20 May 1996, WT/DS2/AB/R, p. 30], WTO Members are free to adopt their own policies aimed at protecting the environment as long as, in so doing, they fulfill their obligations and respect the rights of other Members under the WTO Agreement."

A GATT dispute: The tuna-dolphin dispute

This case still attracts a lot of attention because of its implications for environmental disputes. It was handled under the old GATT dispute settlement procedure. Key questions are:

can one country tell another what its environmental regulations should be? and

do trade rules permit action to be taken against the method used to produce goods (rather than the quality of the goods themselves)?

What was it all about?

In eastern tropical areas of the Pacific Ocean, schools of yellowfin tuna often swim beneath schools of dolphins. When tuna is harvested with purse seine nets, dolphins are trapped in the nets. They often die unless they are released.

The US Marine Mammal Protection Act sets dolphin protection standards for the domestic American fishing fleet and for countries whose fishing boats catch yellowfin tuna in that part of the Pacific Ocean. If a country exporting tuna to the United States cannot prove to US authorities that it meets the dolphin protection standards set out in US law, the US government must embargo all imports of the fish from that country. In this dispute, Mexico was the exporting country concerned. Its exports of tuna to the US were banned. Mexico complained in 1991 under the GATT dispute settlement procedure.

The embargo also applies to "intermediary" countries handling the tuna en route from Mexico to the United States. Often the tuna is processed and canned in an one of these countries. In this dispute, the "intermediary" countries facing the embargo were Costa Rica, Italy, Japan and Spain, and earlier France, the Netherlands Antilles, and the United Kingdom. Others, including Canada, Colombia, the

Republic of Korea, and members of the Association of Southeast Asian Nations (ASEAN), were also named as "intermediaries".

The panel

Mexico asked for a panel in February 1991. A number of "intermediary" countries also expressed an interest. The panel reported to GATT members in September 1991. It concluded:

that the US could not embargo imports of tuna products from Mexico simply because Mexican regulations on the way tuna was produced did not satisfy US regulations. (But the US could apply its regulations on the quality or content of the tuna imported.) This has become known as a "product" versus "process" issue.

that GATT rules did not allow one country to take trade action for the purpose of attempting to enforce its own domestic laws in another country — even to protect animal health or exhaustible natural resources. The term used here is "extra-territoriality".

What was the reasoning behind this ruling? If

the US arguments were accepted, then any country could ban imports of a product from another country merely because the exporting country has different environmental, health and social policies from its own. This would create a virtually open-ended route for any country to apply trade restrictions unilaterally — and to do so not just to enforce its own laws domestically, but to impose its own standards on other countries. The door would be opened to a possible flood of protectionist abuses. This would conflict with the main purpose of the multilateral trading system — to achieve predictability through trade rules.

The panel's task was restricted to examining how GATT rules applied to the issue. It was not asked whether the policy was environmentally correct or not. It suggested that the US policy could be made compatible with GATT rules if members agreed on amendments or reached a decision to waive the rules specially for this issue. That way, the members could negotiate the specific issues, and could set limits that would prevent protectionist abuse.

The panel was also asked to judge the US policy of requiring tuna products to be labelled "dolphin-safe" (leaving to consumers the choice of whether or not to buy the product). It concluded that this did not violate GATT rules because it was designed to prevent deceptive advertising practices on all tuna products, whether imported or domestically produced.

Eco-labelling: good, if it doesn't discriminate

Labelling environmentally-friendly products is an important environmental policy instrument. For the WTO, the key point is that labelling requirements and practices should not discriminate — either between trading partners (most-favoured nation treatment should apply), or between domestically-produced goods or services and imports (national treatment).

One area where the Trade and Environment Committee needs further discussion is how to handle — under the rules of the WTO Technical Barriers to Trade Agreement — labelling used to describe whether *for the way a product is* produced (as distinct from the product itself) is environmentally-friendly.

Transparency: information without too much

paperwork

Like non-discrimination, this is an important WTO principle. Here, WTO members should provide as much information as possible about the environmental policies they have adopted or actions they may take, when these can have a significant impact on trade. They should do this by notifying the WTO, but the task should not be more of a burden than is normally required for other policies affecting trade.

The Trade and Environment Committee says WTO rules do not need changing for this purpose. The WTO Secretariat is to compile from its Central Registry of Notifications all information on trade-related environmental measures that members have submitted. These are to be put in a single database which all WTO members can access

Domestically prohibited goods: dangerous chemicals, etc

This is a concern of a number of developing countries, which are worried that certain hazardous or toxic products are being exported to their markets without them being fully informed about the environmental or public health dangers the products may pose. Developing countries want to be fully informed so as to be in a position to decide whether or not to import them.

A number of international agreements now exist (e.g. the Basel Convention on the Control of Transboundary Movements of Hazardous Wastes and their Disposal, and the London Guidelines for Exchange of Information on Chemicals in International Trade). The WTO's Trade and Environment Committee does not intend to duplicate their work but it also notes that the WTO could play a complementary role.

Liberalization and sustainable development: good for each other

Does freer trade help or hinder environmental protection? The Trade and Environment Committee is analysing the relationship between trade liberalization (including the Uruguay Round commitments) and the protection of the environment. Members say the removal of trade restrictions and distortions can yield benefits both for the multilateral trading system and the environment. Further work is scheduled.

Intellectual property, services: some scope for study

Discussions in the Trade and Environment Committee on these two issues have broken new ground since there was very little understanding of how the rules of the trading system might affect or be affected by environmental policies in these areas.

On services, the committee says further work is needed to examine the relationship between the and environmental protection policies in the sector.

The committee says that the helps countries obtain environmentally-sound technology and products. More work is scheduled on this, including on the relationship between the TRIPS Agreement and the Convention of Biological Diversity

These four subjects were originally included on

the Doha Development Agenda. The carefully-negotiated mandate was for negotiations to start after the 2003 Cancún Ministerial Conference, "on the basis of a decision to be taken, by explicit consensus, at that session on modalities of negotiations". There was no consensus, and the members agreed on 1 August 2004 to proceed with negotiations in only one subject, trade facilitation. The other three were dropped from the Doha agenda.

> See also

Investment and competition: what role for the WTO?

Work in the WTO on investment and competition policy issues originally took the form of specific responses to specific trade policy issues, rather than a look at the broad picture.

Decisions reached at the 1996 Ministerial Conference in Singapore changed the perspective. The ministers decided to set up **two working groups** to look more generally at how trade relates to investment and competition policies.

The working groups' tasks were analytical and exploratory. They would not negotiate new rules or commitments without a clear consensus decision.

The ministers also recognized the work underway in the UN Conference on Trade and Development (UNCTAD) and other international organizations. The working groups were to cooperate with these organizations so as to make best use of available resources and to ensure that development issues are fully taken into account.

An indication of how closely trade is linked with investment is the fact that about one third of the $6.1 trillion total for world trade in goods and services in 1995 was trade within companies — for example between subsidiaries in different countries or between a subsidiary and its headquarters.

The close relationships between trade and investment and competition policy have long been recognized. One of the intentions, when GATT was drafted in the late 1940s, was for rules on investment and competition policy to exist alongside those for trade in goods. (The other two agreements were not completed because the attempt to create an International Trade Organization failed.)

Over the years, GATT and the WTO have increasingly dealt with specific aspects of the relationships. For example, one type of trade covered by the is the supply of services by a foreign company setting up operations in a host country — i.e. through foreign investment. The Trade-Related Investment Measures Agreement says investors' right to use imported goods as inputs should not depend on their export performance.

The same goes for competition policy. GATT and GATS contain rules on monopolies and exclusive service suppliers. The principles have been elaborated considerably in the rules and commitments on telecommunications. The agreements on and services both recognize governments' rights to act against anti-competitive practices, and their rights to work together to limit these practices.

>
>

Transparency in government purchases: towards multilateral rules

The WTO already has an Agreement on Government Procurement. It is plurilateral — only some WTO members have signed it so far. The agreement covers such issues as transparency and non-discrimination.

The decision by WTO ministers at the 1996

Singapore conference did two things. It set up a working group that was multilateral — it included all WTO members. And it focused the group's work on transparency in government procurement practices. The group did not look at preferential treatment for local suppliers, so long as the preferences were not hidden.

The first phase of the group's work was to study transparency in government procurement practices, taking into account national policies. The second phase was to develop elements for inclusion in an agreement.

>

Trade facilitation: a new high profile

Once formal trade barriers come down, other issues become more important. For example, companies need to be able to acquire information on other countries' importing and exporting regulations and how customs procedures are handled. Cutting red-tape at the point where goods enter a country and providing easier access to this kind of information are two ways of "facilitating" trade.

The 1996 Singapore ministerial conference instructed the WTO <u>Goods Council</u> to start exploratory and analytical work "on the simplification of trade procedures in order to assess the scope for WTO rules in this area". Negotiations began after the General Council decision of 1 August 2004.

Chapter – 14

Regional Trade Agreements

The declaration on global electronic commerce adopted by the Second (Geneva) Ministerial Conference on 20 May 1998 urged the WTO General Council to establish a comprehensive work programme to examine all trade-related issues arising from global electronic commerce. The General Council adopted the plan for this work programme on 25 September 1998, initiating discussions on issues of electronic commerce and trade by the Goods, Services and TRIPS (intellectual property) Councils and the Trade and Development Committee.

In the meantime, WTO members also agreed to continue their current practice of not imposing customs duties on electronic transmissions.

There is a clear consensus: all WTO member governments are committed to a narrower set of internationally recognized "core" standards — freedom of association, no forced labour, no child labour, and no discrimination at work (including gender discrimination).

At the 1996 Singapore Ministerial Conference, members defined the WTO's role on this issue, identifying the as the competent body to negotiate labour standards. There is no work on this subject in the WTO's Councils and Committees. However the secretariats of the two organizations work together on technical issues under the banner of "coherence" in global economic policy-making.

However, beyond that it is not easy for them to agree, and the question of international enforcement is a minefield.

Why was this brought to the WTO? What is the debate about?

Four broad questions have been raised inside

and outside the WTO.

The analytical question: if a country has lower standards for labour rights, do its exports gain an unfair advantage? Would this force all countries to lower their standards (the "race to the bottom")?

The response question: if there is a "race to the bottom", should countries only trade with those that have similar labour standards?

The question of rules: Should WTO rules explicitly allow governments to take trade action as a means of putting pressure on other countries to comply?

The institutional question: is the WTO the proper place to discuss and set rules on labour — or to enforce them, including those of the ILO?

In addition, all these points have an underlying question: whether trade actions could be used to impose labour standards, or whether this would simply be an excuse for protectionism. Similar questions are asked about standards, i.e. sanitary and phytosanitary measures, and technical barriers to trade.

The WTO agreements do not deal with labour standards as such.

On the one hand, some countries would like to change this. WTO rules and disciplines, they argue, would provide a powerful incentive for member nations to improve workplace conditions and "international coherence" (the phrase used to describe efforts to ensure policies move in the same direction).

On the other hand, many developing countries believe the issue has no place in the WTO framework. They argue that the campaign to bring labour issues into the WTO is actually a bid by industrial nations to undermine the comparative advantage of lower wage trading partners, and could undermine their ability to raise standards through economic development, particularly if it hampers their ability to trade. They also argue that proposed standards can be too high for them to meet at their level of development. These nations argue that efforts to bring labour standards into the arena of multilateral trade negotiations are little more than a smokescreen for protectionism.

At a more complex legal level is the question of the relationship between the International Labour Organization's standards and the WTO agreements — for example whether or how the ILO's standards can be applied in a way that is consistent with WTO rules.

What has happened in the WTO?

In the WTO, the debate has been hard-fought, particularly in 1996 and 1999. It was at the 1996 Singapore conference that members agreed they were committed to recognized core labour standards, but these should not be used for protectionism. The economic advantage of low-wage countries should not be questioned, but the WTO and ILO secretariats would continue their existing collaboration, the declaration said. The concluding remarks of the chairman, Singapore's trade and industry minister, Mr Yeo Cheow Tong, added that the declaration does not put labour on the WTO's agenda. The countries concerned might continue their pressure for more work to be done in the WTO, but for the time being there are no committees or working parties dealing with the issue.

The issue was also raised at the Seattle Ministerial Conference in 1999, but with no agreement reached. The 2001 Doha Ministerial Conference reaffirmed the Singapore declaration on labour without any specific discussion.

This issue was also indirectly mentioned in the Appellate Body Report (see para. 182) on the dispute initiated by India against the European Communities concerning the conditions for granting of tariff preferences to developing countries.

At the Fourth Ministerial Conference in Doha, Qatar, in November 2001 WTO member governments agreed to launch new negotiations. They also agreed to work on other issues, in particular the implementation of the present agreements. The entire package is called the .

The negotiations take place in the and its subsidiaries, which are usually, either regular councils and committees meeting in "**special sessions**", or specially-created **negotiating groups**. Other work under the work programme takes place in other WTO councils and committees.

The **Fifth Ministerial Conference in Cancún**, Mexico, in September 2003, was intended as a stock-taking meeting where members would agree on how to complete the rest of the negotiations. But the meeting was soured by discord on agricultural issues, including cotton, and ended in deadlock on the "Singapore issues" (). Real progress on the Singapore issues and agriculture was not evident until the early hours of 1 August 2004 with a set of decisions in the General Council (sometimes called the July 2004 package). **The original 1 January 2005** deadline was missed. After that, members unofficially aimed to finish the negotiations **by the end of 2006**, again unsuccessfully. Further progress in narrowing members' differences was made at the Hong Kong Ministerial Conference in December 2005, but some gaps remained unbridgeable and Director-General Pascal Lamy suspended the negotiations in July 2006. Efforts then focused on trying to achieve a breakthrough in early 2007.

See also:
>
>
>

There are 19-21 subjects listed in the Doha Declaration, depending on whether to count the "rules" subjects as one or three. Most of them involve negotiations; other work includes actions under "implementation", analysis and monitoring. This is an unofficial explanation of what the declaration mandates (listed with the declaration's paragraphs that refer to them):

Implementation-related issues and concerns (par 12)

"Implementation" is short-hand for developing countries' problems in implementing the current

WTO Agreements, i.e. the agreements arising from the Uruguay Round negotiations.

No area of WTO work received more attention or generated more controversy during nearly three years of hard bargaining before the Doha Ministerial Conference. Around 100 issues were raised during that period. The result was a two-pronged approach:

More than 40 items under 12 headings were settled at or before the Doha conference, for immediate delivery.

The vast majority of the remaining items immediately became the subject of negotiations.

This was spelt out in a separate ministerial decision on implementation, combined with paragraph 12 of the main Doha Declaration.

The **implementation decision** includes the following (detailed explanations can be seen on the WTO website):

General Agreement on Tariffs and Trade (GATT)

Balance-of-payments exception: clarifying less

stringent conditions in GATT for developing countries if they restrict imports in order to protect their balance-of-payments.

Market-access commitments: clarifying eligibility to negotiate or be consulted on quota allocation.

Agriculture

Rural development and food security for developing countries

Least-developed and net food-importing developing countries

Export credits, export credit guarantees or insurance programmes

Tariff rate quotas

Sanitary and phytosanitary (SPS) measures

More time for developing countries to comply with other countries' new SPS measures

"Reasonable interval" between publication of a country's new SPS measure and its entry into force

Equivalence: putting into practice the principle

that governments should accept that different measures used by other governments can be equivalent to their own measures for providing the same level of health protection for food, animals and plants.

Review of the SPS Agreement

Developing countries' participation in setting international SPS standards

Financial and technical assistance

Textiles and clothing

"Effective" use of the agreement's provisions on early integration of products into normal GATT rules, and elimination of quotas.

Restraint in anti-dumping actions.

The possibility of examining governments' new rules of origin.

Members to consider favourable quota treatment for small suppliers and least-developed countries, and larger quotas in general.

Technical barriers to trade

Technical assistance for least-developed

countries, and reviews of technical assistance in general.

When possible, a six-month "reasonable interval" for developing countries to adapt to new measures.

The WTO director-general encouraged to continue efforts to help developing countries participate in setting international standards.

Trade-related investment measures (TRIMs)

The Goods Council is "to consider positively" requests from least-developed countries to extend the seven-year transition period for eliminating measures that are inconsistent with the agreement.

Anti-dumping (GATT Article 6)

No second anti-dumping investigation within a year unless circumstances have changed.

How to put into operation a special provision for developing countries (Article 15 of the Anti-Dumping Agreement), which recognizes that developed countries must give "special regard" to the situation of developing countries when considering applying anti-dumping measures.

Clarification sought on the time period for determining whether the volume of dumped imported products is negligible, and therefore no anti-dumping action should be taken.

Annual reviews of the agreement's implementation to be improved.

Customs valuation (GATT Article 7)

Extending the deadline for developing countries to implement the agreement

Dealing with fraud: how to cooperate in exchanging information, including on export values

Rules of origin

Completing the harmonization of rules of origin among member governments

Dealing with interim arrangements in the transition to the new, harmonized rules of origin.

Subsidies and countervailing measures

Sorting out how to determine whether some developing countries meet the test of being below US$1,000 per capita GNP allowing them to pay subsidies that require the recipient to export.

Noting proposed new rules allowing developing countries to subsidize under programmes that have "legitimate development goals" without having to face countervailing or other action.

Review of provisions on countervailing duty investigations.

Reaffirming that least-developed countries are exempt from the ban on export subsidies.

Directing the Subsidies Committee to extend the transition period for certain developing countries.

Trade-related aspects of intellectual property rights (TRIPS)

"Non-violation" complaints: the unresolved question of how to deal with possible TRIPS disputes involving loss of an expected benefit even if the TRIPS Agreement has not actually been violated.

Technology transfer to least-developed countries

Cross-cutting issues

Which special and differential treatment provisions are mandatory? What are the implications of making mandatory those that are currently non-binding?

How can special and differential treatment provisions be made more effective?

How can special and differential treatment be incorporated in the new negotiations?

Developed countries are urged to grant preferences in a generalized and non-discriminatory manner, i.e. to all developing countries rather than to a selected group.

Outstanding implementation issues

To be handled under paragraph 12 of the main Doha Declaration.

Final provisions

The WTO Director-General is to ensure that WTO technical assistance gives priority to helping developing countries implement existing WTO obligations, and to increase their capacity to participate more effectively in future negotiations.

The WTO Secretariat is to cooperate more closely with other international organizations so that technical assistance is more efficient and effective.

The implementation decision is tied into the **main Doha Declaration**, where ministers agreed on a future work programme to deal with unsettled implementation questions. "Negotiations on outstanding implementation issues shall be an integral part of the Work Programme" in the coming years, they declared.

In the declaration, the ministers established a two-track approach. Those issues for which there was an agreed negotiating mandate in the declaration would be dealt with under the terms of that mandate.

Those implementation issues where there is no mandate to negotiate, would be the taken up as "a matter of priority" by relevant WTO councils and committees. These bodies were to report on their progress to the Trade Negotiations Committee by the end of 2002 for "appropriate action".

Agriculture(par 13, 14)

Negotiations on agriculture began in early 2000, under Article 20 of the WTO Agriculture Agreement. By November 2001 and the Doha Ministerial Conference, 121 governments had submitted a large number of negotiating proposals.

These negotiations have continued, but now with the mandate given by the Doha Declaration, which also includes a series of deadlines. The declaration builds on the work already undertaken, confirms and elaborates the objectives, and sets a timetable. Agriculture is now part of the single undertaking in which virtually all the linked negotiations were to end by 1 January 2005, now with the unofficial target of the end of 2006.

The declaration reconfirms the long-term objective already agreed in the present WTO Agreement: to establish a fair and market-oriented trading system through a programme of fundamental reform. The programme encompasses strengthened rules, and specific commitments on government support and protection for agriculture. The purpose is to correct and prevent restrictions and distortions in world agricultural markets.

Without prejudging the outcome, member governments commit themselves to comprehensive negotiations aimed at:

market access: substantial reductions

exports subsidies: reductions of, with a view to phasing out, all forms of these (in the 1 August 2004 "framework" members agreed to eliminate export subsidies by a date to be negotiated)

domestic support: substantial reductions for supports that distort trade (in the 1 August 2004 "framework", developed countries pledged to slash trade-distorting domestic subsidies by 20% from the first day any Doha Agenda agreement is implemented.

The declaration makes special and differential treatment for developing countries integral throughout the negotiations, both in countries' new commitments and in any relevant new or revised rules and disciplines. It says the outcome should be effective in practice and should enable developing countries to meet their needs, in particular in food security and rural development.

The ministers also take note of the non-trade concerns (such as environmental protection, food security, rural development, etc) reflected in the negotiating proposals already submitted. They confirm that the negotiations will take these into account, as provided for in the Agriculture Agreement.

A first step along the road to final agreement was reached on 1 August 2004 when members agreed on a "framework" (Annex A of the General Council decision).

The negotiations take place in **"special sessions" of the Agriculture Committee**.

> >

Key dates: agriculture

Start: **early 2000**

"Framework" agreed: **1 August 2004**.

Formulas and other "modalities" for countries' commitments: originally 31 March 2003, **now by 6th Ministerial Conference, 2005** (in Hong Kong, China)

Countries' comprehensive draft commitments and stock taking: originally by 5th Ministerial Conference, 2003 (in Mexico)

Deadline: Now none. Originally by 1 January 2005, then unofficially by end of 2006. Part of single undertaking

Services (par 15)

Negotiations on services were already almost two years old when they were incorporated into the new Doha agenda.

The WTO General Agreement on Trade in Services (GATS) commits member governments to undertake negotiations on specific issues and to enter into successive rounds of negotiations to progressively liberalize trade in services. The first round had to start no later than five years from 1995.

Accordingly, the services negotiations started officially in early 2000 under the Council for Trade in Services. In March 2001, the Services Council fulfilled a key element in the negotiating mandate by establishing the negotiating guidelines and procedures.

The Doha Declaration endorses the work already done, reaffirms the negotiating guidelines and procedures, and establishes some key elements of the timetable including, most importantly, the deadline for concluding the negotiations as part of a single undertaking.

The negotiations take place in **"special sessions" of the Services Council** and **regular meetings** of its relevant subsidiary committees or working parties.

>>

Key dates: services

Start: **early 2000**

Negotiating guidelines and procedures: **March 2001**

Initial requests for market access: **by 30 June**

2002

Initial offers of market access: **by 31 March 2003**

Stock taking: originally 5th Ministerial Conference, 2003 (in Mexico)

Revised market-access offers: **by 31 May 2005**

Deadline: Now none. Originally by 1 January 2005, then unofficially end of 2006. Part of single undertaking

Market access for non-agricultural products (par 16)

The ministers agreed to launch tariff-cutting negotiations on all non-agricultural products. The aim is "to reduce, or as appropriate eliminate tariffs, including the reduction or elimination of tariff peaks, high tariffs, and tariff escalation, as well as non-tariff barriers, in particular on products of export interest to developing countries". These negotiations shall take fully into account the special needs and interests of developing and least-developed countries, and recognize that these countries do not need to match or reciprocate in full tariff-reduction commitments by other participants.

At the start, participants have to reach agreement on how ("modalities") to conduct the tariff-cutting exercise (in the Tokyo Round, the participants used an agreed mathematical formula to cut tariffs across the board; in the Uruguay Round, participants negotiated cuts product by product). The agreed procedures would include studies and capacity-building measures that would help least-developed countries participate effectively in the negotiations. Back in Geneva, negotiators decided that the "modalities" should be agreed by 31 May 2003. When that date was missed, members agreed on 1 August 2004 on a new target: the Hong Kong Ministerial Conference in December 2005.

While average customs duties are now at their lowest levels after eight GATT Rounds, certain tariffs continue to restrict trade, especially on exports of developing countries — for instance "tariff peaks", which are relatively high tariffs, usually on "sensitive" products, amidst generally low tariff levels. For industrialized countries, tariffs of 15% and above are generally recognized as "tariff peaks".

Another example is "tariff escalation", in which higher import duties are applied on semi-processed products than on raw materials, and higher still on finished products. This practice protects domestic processing industries and discourages the development of processing activity in the countries where raw materials originate.

The negotiations take place in a **Market Access Negotiating Group**.

>>
>

Key dates: market access

Start: **January 2002**

Stock taking: **5th Ministerial Conference, 2003** (in Mexico)

Deadline: Now none. Originally by 1 January 2005, now unofficially by end 2006. Part of single undertaking

Trade-related aspects of intellectual property

rights (TRIPS)(pars 17-19)

TRIPS and public health. In the declaration, ministers stress that it is important to implement and interpret the TRIPS Agreement in a way that supports public health — by promoting both access to existing medicines and the creation of new medicines. They refer to their separate declaration on this subject.

This separate declaration on TRIPS and public health is designed to respond to concerns about the possible implications of the TRIPS Agreement for access to medicines.

It emphasizes that the TRIPS Agreement does not and should not prevent member governments from acting to protect public health. It affirms governments' right to use the agreement's flexibilities in order to avoid any reticence the governments may feel.

The separate declaration clarifies some of the forms of flexibility available, in particular compulsory licensing and parallel importing. (For an explanation of these issues, go to the main TRIPS pages on the WTO website)

For the Doha agenda, this separate declaration sets two specific task. The **TRIPS Council** has to find a solution to the problems countries may face in making use of compulsory licensing if they have too little or no pharmaceutical manufacturing capacity, reporting to the General Council on this by the end of 2002.(this was achieved in August, 2003, see section of the "Agreements" chapter.) The declaration also extends the deadline for least-developed countries to apply provisions on pharmaceutical patents until 1 January 2016.

Geographical indications — the registration system. Geographical indications are place names (in some countries also words associated with a place) used to identify products with particular characteristics because they come from specific places. The WTO TRIPS Council has already started work on a multilateral registration system for geographical indications for wines and spirits. The Doha Declaration sets a deadline for completing the negotiations: the Fifth Ministerial Conference in 2003.

These negotiations take place in **"special**

sessions" of the TRIPS Council.

Geographical indications — extending the "higher level of protection" to other products. The TRIPS Agreement provides a higher level of protection to geographical indications for wines and spirits. This means they should be protected even if there is no risk of misleading consumers or unfair competition. A number of countries want to negotiate extending this higher level to other products. Others oppose the move, and the debate in the TRIPS Council has included the question of whether the relevant provisions of the TRIPS Agreement provide a mandate for extending coverage beyond wines and spirits.

The Doha Declaration notes that the **TRIPS Council** will handle this under the declaration's paragraph 12 (which deals with implementation issues). Paragraph 12 offers two tracks: "(a) where we provide a specific negotiating mandate in this Declaration, the relevant implementation issues shall be addressed under that mandate; (b) the other outstanding implementation issues shall be addressed as a matter of priority by the relevant WTO bodies, which shall report to the Trade Negotiations Committee [TNC], established under paragraph 46 below, by the end of 2002 for appropriate action."

In papers circulated at the Ministerial Conference, member governments expressed different interpretations of this mandate.

Argentina said it understands "there is no agreement to negotiate the 'other outstanding implementation issues' referred to under (b) and that, by the end of 2002, consensus will be required in order to launch any negotiations on these issues".

Bulgaria, the Czech Republic, EU, Hungary, India, Liechtenstein, Kenya, Mauritius, Nigeria, Pakistan, the Slovak Republic, Slovenia, Sri Lanka, Switzerland, Thailand and Turkey argued that there is a clear mandate to negotiate immediately.

Reviews of TRIPS provisions. Two reviews have been taking place in the TRIPS Council, as required by the TRIPS Agreement: a review of Article 27.3(b) which deals with patentability or non-patentability of plant and animal inventions, and the protection of plant varieties; and a review of the entire TRIPS Agreement (required by Article 71.1).

The Doha Declaration says that work in the **TRIPS Council** on these reviews or any other implementation issue should also look at: the relationship between the TRIPS Agreement and the UN Convention on Biodiversity; the protection of traditional knowledge and folklore; and other relevant new developments that member governments raise in the review of the TRIPS Agreement. It adds that the TRIPS Council's work on these topics is to be guided by the TRIPS Agreement's objectives (Article 7) and principles (Article 8), and must take development fully into account.

>

Key dates: intellectual property

Report to the General Council — solution on compulsory licensing and lack of pharmaceutical production capacity: originally by end of 2002, decision agreed **30 April 2003.**

Report to TNC — action on outstanding

implementation issues under par 12: **by end of 2002 (missed)**

Deadline — negotiations on geographical indications registration system (wines and spirits): **by 5th Ministerial Conference, 2003** (in Mexico) **(missed)**

Deadline — negotiations specifically mandated in Doha Declaration: now none. Originally by 1 January 2005, then unofficially by end 2006. Part of single undertaking

Least-developed countries to apply pharmaceutical patent provisions: **2016**

The four 'Singapore' issues: no negotiations until …

For

trade and **investment**, trade and **competition policy**, **transparency in government procurement** and **trade facilitation**, the 2001 Doha declaration does not launch negotiations immediately. It says "negotiations will take place after the Fifth Session of the Ministerial Conference on the basis of a decision to be taken, by explicit consensus, at that session on modalities of negotiations [i.e. how the negotiations are to be conducted]." But consensus eluded members on negotiating the four subjects. Finally agreement was reached on 1 August 2004 to negotiate **trade facilitation** alone. The three other subjects were droppe d from the Doha agenda

Relationship between trade and investment ([pars 20-22](#))

This is a "" i.e. a working group set up by the 1996 Singapore Ministerial Conference has been studying it.

In the period up to the 2003 Ministerial Conference, the declaration instructs the **working group** to focus on clarifying the scope and definition of the issues, transparency, non-discrimination, ways of preparing negotiated commitments, development provisions, exceptions and balance-of-payments safeguards, consultation and dispute settlement. The negotiated commitments would be modelled on those made in services, which specify where commitments are being made — "positive lists" — rather than making broad commitments and listing exceptions.

The declaration also spells out a number of principles such as the need to balance the interests of countries where foreign investment originates and where it is invested, countries' right to regulate investment, development, public interest and individual countries' specific circumstances. It also emphasizes support and technical cooperation for developing and least-developed countries, and coordination with other international organizations such as the UN Conference on Trade and Development (UNCTAD).

Since the 1 August 2004 decision, this subject has been dropped from the Doha agenda.

> statement: chairman's understanding of the mandate ...
>

Key dates: trade and investment

Continuing work in working group with defined agenda: **to 5th Ministerial Conference, 2003 (in Mexico)**

Negotiations: after 5th Ministerial Conference, 2003 (in Mexico) subject to "explicit consensus" on modalities with deadline: by 1 January 2005, part of single undertaking. But no consensus; **dropped from Doha agenda in 1 August 2004**

decision

Interaction between trade and competition policy (pars 23-25)

This is another "Singapore issue", with a working group set up in 1996 to study the subject.

In the period up to the 2003 Ministerial Conference, the declaration instructs the **working group** to focus on clarifying:

core principles including transparency, non-discrimination and procedural fairness, and provisions on "hardcore" cartels (i.e. cartels that are formally set up)

ways of handling voluntary cooperation on competition policy among WTO member governments

support for progressive reinforcement of competition institutions in developing countries through capacity building

The declaration says the work must take full account of developmental needs. It includes technical cooperation and capacity building, on such topics as policy analysis and development, so that developing countries are better placed to evaluate the implications of closer multilateral cooperation for various developmental objectives. Cooperation with other organizations such as the UN Conference on Trade and Development (UNCTAD) is also included.

Since the 1 August 2004 decision, this subject has been dropped from the Doha agenda.

> statement: <u>chairman's understanding of the mandate</u> ... >

Key dates: trade and competition policy

Continuing work in working group with defined agenda: **to 5th Ministerial Conference, 2003 (in Mexico)**

Negotiations: after 5th Ministerial Conference, 2003 (in Mexico) subject to "explicit consensus" on modalities with deadline: by 1 January 2005, part of single undertaking. But no consensus; **dropped from Doha agenda in 1 August 2004 decision**

Transparency in government procurement (<u>par</u>

26)

A third "Singapore issue" that was handled by a **working group** set up by the Singapore Ministerial Conference in 1996.

The Doha Declaration says that the "negotiations shall be limited to the transparency aspects and therefore will not restrict the scope for countries to give preferences to domestic supplies and suppliers" — it is separate from the plurilateral Government Procurement Agreement.

The declaration also stresses development concerns, technical assistance and capacity building.

Since the 1 August 2004 decision, this subject has been dropped from the Doha agenda.

> statement: chairman's understanding of the mandate ....
>

Key dates: government procurement (transparency)

Continuing work in working group with defined agenda: **to 5th Ministerial Conference, 2003**

(in Mexico)

Negotiations: after 5th Ministerial Conference, 2003 (in Mexico) subject to "explicit consensus" on modalities with deadline: by 1 January 2005, part of single undertaking. But no consensus; **dropped from Doha agenda in 1 August 2004 Decision.**

Trade facilitation (par 27)

A fourth "Singapore issue" kicked off by the 1996 Ministerial Conference.

The declaration recognizes the case for "further expediting the movement, release and clearance of goods, including goods in transit, and the need for enhanced technical assistance and capacity building in this area".

In the period until the Fifth Ministerial Conference in 2003, the **WTO Goods Council**, which had been working on this subject since 1997, "shall review and as appropriate, clarify and improve relevant aspects of Articles 5 ('Freedom of Transit'), 8 ('Fees and Formalities Connected with Importation and Exportation') and 10 ('Publication and Administration of

Trade Regulations') of the General Agreement on Tariffs and Trade (GATT 1994) and identify the trade facilitation needs and priorities of Members, in particular developing and least-developed countries".

Those issues were cited in the 1 August 2004 decision that broke the Cancún deadlock. Members agreed to start negotiations on trade facilitation, but not the three other Singapore issues.

> statement: chairman's understanding of the mandate .... >

Key dates: trade facilitation

Continuing work in Goods Council with defined agenda: **to 5th Ministerial Conference, 2003** (in Mexico)

Negotiations: **after 5th Ministerial Conference, 2003** (in Mexico) subject to "explicit consensus" on modalities, agreed in 1 August 2004 Decision.

Deadline: Now none. Originally by 1 January 2005, then unofficially end of 2006. Part of single undertaking

WTO rules: anti-dumping and subsidies (par 28)

The ministers agreed to negotiations on the Anti-Dumping (GATT Article 6) and Subsidies agreements. The aim is to clarify and improve disciplines while preserving the basic, concepts, principles of these agreements, and taking into account the needs of developing and least-developed participants.

In overlapping negotiating phases, participants first indicated which provisions of these two agreements they think should be the subject of clarification and improvement in the next phase of negotiations. The ministers mention specifically fisheries subsidies as one sector important to developing countries and where participants should aim to clarify and improve WTO disciplines.

Negotiations take place in the **Rules Negotiating Group**.

>
>
>

Key dates: anti-dumping, subsidies

Start: **January 2002**

Stock taking: **5th Ministerial Conference, 2003** (in Mexico)

Deadline: Now none. Originally by 1 January 2005, then unofficially end of 2006. Part of single undertaking

WTO rules: regional trade agreements (par 29)

WTO rules say regional trade agreements have to meet certain conditions. But interpreting the wording of these rules has proved controversial, and has been a central element in the work of the Regional Trade Agreements Committee. As a result, since 1995 the committee has failed to complete its assessments of whether individual trade agreements conform with WTO provisions.

This is now an important challenge, particularly when nearly all member governments are parties to regional agreements, are negotiating them, or are considering negotiating them. In the Doha Declaration, members agreed to negotiate a solution, giving due regard to the role that these agreements can play in fostering development.

The declaration mandates negotiations aimed at "clarifying and improving disciplines and procedures under the existing WTO provisions applying to regional trade agreements. The negotiations shall take into account the developmental aspects of regional trade agreements."

These negotiations fell into the general timetable established for virtually all negotiations under the Doha Declaration. The original deadline of 1 January 2005 was missed and the current unofficial aim is to finish the talks by the end of 2006. The 2003 Fifth Ministerial Conference in Mexico was intended to take stock of progress, provide any necessary political guidance, and take decisions as necessary.

Negotiations take place in the **Rules Negotiating Group**.

>

>

Key dates: regional trade

Start: **January 2002**

Stock taking: **5th Ministerial Conference, 2003** (in Mexico)

Deadline: Now none. Originally by 1 January 2005, then unofficially end of 2006. Part of single undertaking

Dispute Settlement Understanding (par 30)

The 1994 Marrakesh Ministerial Conference mandated WTO member governments to conduct a review of the Dispute Settlement Understanding (DSU, the WTO agreement on dispute settlement) within four years of the entry into force of the WTO Agreement (i.e. by 1 January 1999).

The Dispute Settlement Body (DSB) started the review in late 1997, and held a series of informal discussions on the basis of proposals and issues that members identified. Many, if not all, members clearly felt that improvements should be made to the understanding. However, the DSB could not reach a consensus on the results of the review.

The Doha Declaration mandates negotiations and states (in par 47) that these will not be part of the single undertaking — i.e. that they will not be tied to the overall success or failure of the other negotiations mandated by the declaration. Originally set to conclude by May 2003, the negotiations are continuing without a deadline.

Negotiations take place in **"special sessions" of the Dispute Settlement Body**.

> [more on Dispute Settlement Understanding negotiations](#)

Key dates: disputes understanding

Start: **January 2002**

Deadline: originally by May 2003, currently no deadline, separate from single undertaking

Trade and environment
([pars 31-33](#))

New negotiations

Multilateral environmental agreements. Ministers agreed to launch negotiations on the relationship between existing WTO rules and specific trade obligations set out in multilateral environmental agreements. The negotiations will address how WTO rules are to apply to WTO members that are parties to environmental agreements, in particular to clarify the relationship between trade measures taken under the environmental agreements and WTO rules.

So far no measure affecting trade taken under an environmental agreement has been challenged in the GATT-WTO system.

Information exchange. Ministers agreed to negotiate procedures for regular information exchange between secretariats of multilateral environmental agreements and the WTO. Currently, the Trade and Environment Committee holds an information session with different secretariats of the multilateral environmental agreements once or twice a year to discuss the trade-related provisions in these environmental agreements and also their dispute settlement mechanisms. The new information exchange procedures may expand the scope of existing cooperation.

Observer status. Overall, the situation concerning the granting of observer status in the WTO to other international governmental organizations is currently blocked for political reasons. The negotiations aim to develop criteria for observership in WTO.

Trade barriers on environmental goods and services. Ministers also agreed to negotiations on the reduction or elimination of tariff and non-tariff barriers to environmental goods and services. Examples of environmental goods and services are catalytic converters, air filters or consultancy services on wastewater management.

Fisheries subsidies. Ministers agreed to clarify and improve WTO rules that apply to fisheries subsidies. The issue of fisheries subsidies has been studied in the Trade and Environment Committee for several years. Some studies demonstrate these subsidies can be environmentally damaging if they lead to too many fishermen chasing too few fish.

Negotiations on these issues, including concepts of what are the relevant environmental goods and services, take place in **"special sessions" of the Trade and Environment Committee**. Negotiations on market access for environmental goods and services take place in the **Market**

Access Negotiating Group and **Services Council "special sessions"**.

Work in the committee

Ministers instructed the **Trade and Environment Committee**, in pursuing work on all items on its agenda, to pay particular attention to the following areas:

The effect of environmental measures on market access, especially for developing countries.

"Win-win-win" situations: when eliminating or reducing trade restrictions and distortions would benefit trade, the environment and development.

Intellectual property. Paragraph 19 of the Ministerial Declaration mandates the TRIPs Council to continue clarifying the relationship between the TRIPS Agreement and the Biological Diversity Convention. Ministers also ask the Trade and Environment Committee to continue to look at the relevant provisions of the TRIPS agreement.

Environmental labelling requirements. The Trade and Environment Committee is to look at the impact of eco-labelling on trade and examine whether existing WTO rules stand in the way of eco-labelling policies. Parallel discussions are to take place in the Technical Barriers to Trade (TBT) Committee.

For all these issues: when working on these (market access, "win-win-win" situations, intellectual property and environmental labelling), the Trade and Environment Committee should identify WTO rules that would need to be clarified.

General: ministers recognize the importance of technical assistance and capacity building programmes for developing countries in the trade and environment area. They also encourage members to share expertise and experience on national environmental reviews.

>

Key dates: environment

Committee reports to ministers: **5th and 6th Ministerial Conferences, 2003 and 2005** (in Mexico and Hong Kong, China)

Negotiations stock taking: **5th Ministerial Conference, 2003** (in Mexico)

Negotiations deadline: Deadline: Now none. Originally by 1 January 2005, then unofficially end of 2006. Part of single undertaking

Electronic commerce (par 34)

The Doha Declaration endorses the work already done on electronic commerce and instructs the **General Council** to consider the most appropriate institutional arrangements for handling the work programme, and to report on further progress to the Fifth Ministerial Conference.

The declaration on electronic commerce from the Second Ministerial Conference in Geneva, 1998, said that WTO members will continue their practice of not imposing customs duties on electronic transmissions. The Doha Declaration states that members will continue this practice until the Fifth Ministerial Conference.

>

Key date: electronic commerce

Report on further progress: **5th Ministerial Conference, 2003** (in Mexico)

Small economies (par 35)

Small economies face specific challenges in their participation in world trade, for example lack of economy of scale or limited natural resources.

The Doha Declaration mandates the **General Council** to examine these problems and to make recommendations to the next Ministerial Conference as to what trade-related measures could improve the integration of small economies.

>

Key date: small economies

Recommendations: **5th and 6th Ministerial Conferences, 2003 and 2005** (in Mexico and Hong Kong, China)

Trade, debt and finance (par 36)

Many developing countries face serious external debt problems and have been through financial crises. WTO ministers decided in Doha to establish a **Working Group on Trade, Debt and Finance** to look at how trade-related measures can contribute to find a durable solution to these problems. This working group will report to the General Council which will in turn report to the next Ministerial Conference.

Key date: debt and finance

General Council report: **5th and 6th Ministerial Conferences, 2003 and 2005** (in Mexico and Hong Kong, China)

Trade and technology transfer (par 37)

A number of provisions in the WTO agreements mention the need for a transfer of technology to take place between developed and developing countries.

However, it is not clear how such a transfer takes place in practice and if specific measures might be taken within the WTO to encourage such flows of technology.

WTO ministers decided in Doha to establish a **working group** to examine the issue. The working group will report to the General Council which itself will report to the next Ministerial Conference.

Key date: technology transfer

General Council report: **5th and 6th Ministerial Conferences, 2003 and 2005** (in Mexico and Hong Kong, China)

Technical cooperation and capacity building (pars 38-41)

Through various paragraphs of the Doha Declaration, WTO member governments have made new commitments on technical cooperation and capacity building.

For example, the section on the relationship between trade and investment includes a call (par 21) for enhanced support for technical assistance and capacity building in this area.

Within the specific heading "technical cooperation and capacity building", paragraph 41 lists all the references to commitments on technical cooperation within the Doha Declaration: paragraphs 16 (market access for non-agricultural products), 21 (trade and investment), 24 (trade and competition policy), 26 (transparency in government procurement),

27 (trade facilitation), 33 (environment), 38-40 (technical cooperation and capacity building), 42 and 43 (least-developed countries). (Paragraph 2 in the preamble is also cited.)

Under this heading (i.e. pars 38-41), WTO member governments reaffirm all technical cooperation and capacity building commitments made throughout the declaration and add general commitments:

The Secretariat, in coordination with other relevant agencies, is to encourage WTO developing-country members to consider trade as a main element for reducing poverty and to include trade measures in their development strategies.

The agenda set out in the Doha Declaration gives priority to small, vulnerable, and transition economies, as well as to members and observers that do not have permanent delegations in Geneva.

Technical assistance must be delivered by the WTO and other relevant international organizations within a coherent policy framework.

The **Director-General** reported to the **General Council** in December 2002 and to the **Fifth Ministerial Conference** on the implementation and adequacy of these new commitments.

Following the declaration's instructions to develop a plan ensuring long-term funding for WTO technical assistance, the **General Council** adopted on 20 December 2001 (one month after the Doha conference) a new budget that increased technical assistance funding by 80% and established a Doha Development Agenda Global Trust Fund. The fund now has an annual budget of 24 million Swiss francs.

>

Key dates: technical cooperation

Technical assistance funding raised 80%; Development Agenda Global Trust Fund set up: **December 2001**

Director-General reports to General Council: **December 2002**

Director-General reports to ministers: **5th and 6th Ministerial Conferences, 2003 and 2005** (in Mexico and Hong Kong, China)

Least-developed countries (pars 42, 43)

Many developed countries have now significantly decreased or actually scrapped tariffs on imports from least-developed countries (LDCs).

In the Doha declaration, WTO **member governments** commit themselves to the objective of duty-free, quota-free market access for LDCs' products and to consider additional measures to improve market access for these exports.

Members also agree to try to ensure that least-developed countries can negotiate WTO membership faster and more easily.

Some technical assistance is targeted specifically for least-developed countries. The Doha Declaration urges **WTO member donors** to significantly increase their contributions.

In addition, the **Sub-Committee for LDCs** (a subsidiary body of the WTO Committee on Trade and Development) designed a work programme un February 2002, as instructed by the Doha Declaration, taking into account the parts of the declaration related to trade that was issued at the UN LDC Conference.

>>

Key date: least-developed countries

Reports to: **General Council: July 2002, 5th and 6th Ministerial Conferences, 2003 and 2005** (in Mexico and Hong Kong, China)

Special and differential treatment (par 44)

The WTO agreements contain special provisions which give developing countries special rights. These special provisions include, for example, longer time periods for implementing agreements and commitments or measures to increase trading opportunities for developing countries.

In the Doha Declaration, member governments agree that all special and differential treatment provisions should be reviewed with a view to strengthening them and making them more precise.

More specifically, the declaration (together with the Decision on Implementation-Related Issues and Concerns) mandates the **Trade and Development Committee** to identify which of those special and differential treatment provisions are mandatory, and to consider the implications of making mandatory those which are currently non-binding.

The Decision on Implementation-Related Issues and Concerns instructed the committee to make its recommendations for the **General Council** before July 2002. But because members needed more time, this was postponed to the end of July 2005.

>

Key date: special and differential treatment

Recommendations to General Council: **July 2002, July 2005**

Cancún 2003, Hong Kong 2005

The Doha agenda set a number of tasks to be completed before or at the Fifth Ministerial Conference in Cancún, Mexico, 10–14 September 2003. On the eve of the conference, on 30 August, agreement was reached on the TRIPS and public health issue. However, a number of the deadlines were missed, including "modalities" for agriculture and the non-agricultural market access negotiations, reform of the Dispute Settlement Understanding, and recommendations on special and differential treatment. Nor were members near to agreement on the multilateral geographical indications register for wines and spirits, due to be completed in Cancún.

Although Cancún saw delegations move closer to consensus on a number of key issues, members remained deeply divided over a number of issues, including the "Singapore" issues — launching negotiations on investment, competition policy, transparency in government procurement, and trade facilitation — and agriculture.

The conference ended without consensus. Ten months later, the deadlock was broken in Geneva when the General Council agreed on the "July package" in the early hours of 1 August 2004, which kicked off negotiations in trade facilitation but not the three other Singapore issues. The delay meant the 1 January 2005 deadline for finishing the talks could not be met. Unofficially, members aimed to complete the next phase of the negotiations at the Hong Kong Ministerial Conference, 13–18 December 2005, including full "modalities" in agriculture and market access for non-agricultural products, and to finish the talks by the end of the following year.

the **WTO agreements** contain **special provisions** on developing countries

the is the main body focusing on work in this

area in the WTO, with some others dealing with specific topics such as trade and debt, and technology transfer

the **WTO Secretariat** provides (mainly training of various kinds) for developing countries.

In the agreements: more time, better terms

The WTO agreements include numerous provisions giving developing and least-developed countries special rights or extra leniency — "special and differential treatment". Among these are provisions that allow developed countries to treat developing countries more favourably than other WTO members.

The General Agreement on Tariffs and Trade (GATT, which deals with trade in goods) has a special section (Part 4) on Trade and Development which includes provisions on the concept of non-reciprocity in trade negotiations between developed and developing countries — when developed countries grant trade concessions to developing countries they should not expect the developing countries to make matching offers in return.

Both GATT and the General Agreement on Trade in Services (GATS) allow developing countries some preferential treatment.

Other measures concerning developing countries in the WTO agreements include:

extra time for developing countries to fulfil their commitments (in many of the WTO agreements)

provisions designed to increase developing countries' **trading opportunities** through greater market access (e.g. in , , technical barriers to trade)

provisions requiring WTO members to **safeguard the interests** of developing countries when adopting some domestic or international measures (e.g. in anti-dumping, safeguards, technical barriers to trade)

provisions for various **means of helping** developing countries (e.g. to deal with commitments on animal and plant health standards, technical standards, and in strengthening their domestic telecommunications sectors).

Legal assistance: a Secretariat service

The WTO Secretariat has special legal advisers for assisting developing countries in any WTO dispute and for giving them legal counsel. The service is offered by the WTO's Training and Technical Cooperation Institute. Developing countries regularly make use of it.

Furthermore, in 2001, 32 WTO governments set up an Advisory Centre on WTO law. Its members consist of countries contributing to the funding, and those receiving legal advice. All least-developed countries are automatically eligible for advice. Other developing countries and transition economies have to be fee-paying members in order to receive advice.

Least-developed countries: special focus

The receive extra attention in the WTO. All the WTO agreements recognize that they must benefit from the greatest possible flexibility, and better-off members must make extra efforts to lower import barriers on least-developed countries' exports.

Since the Uruguay Round agreements were signed in 1994, several decisions in favour of least-developed countries have been taken.

Meeting in Singapore in 1996, WTO ministers agreed on a "Plan of Action for Least-Developed Countries". This included technical assistance to enable them to participate better in the multilateral system and a pledge from developed countries to improved market access for least-developed countries' products.

A year later, in October 1997, six international organizations — the International Monetary Fund, the International Trade Centre, the United Nations Conference for Trade and Development, the United Nations Development Programme, the World Bank and the WTO — launched the "Integrated Framework", a joint technical assistance programme exclusively for least-developed countries.

In 2002, the WTO adopted a work programme for least-developed countries. It contains several broad elements: improved market access; more technical assistance; support for agencies working on the diversification of least-developed countries' economies; help in following the work of the WTO; and a speedier membership process for least-developed countries negotiating to join the WTO.

At the same time, more and more member governments have unilaterally scrapped import duties and import quotas on all exports from least-developed countries.

A 'maison' in Geneva: being present is

important, but not easy for all

The WTO's official business takes place mainly in Geneva. So do the unofficial contacts that can be equally important. But having a permanent office of representatives in Geneva can be expensive. Only about one third of the 30 or so least-developed countries in the WTO have permanent offices in Geneva, and they cover all United Nations activities as well as the WTO.

As a result of the negotiations to locate the WTO headquarters in Geneva, the Swiss government has agreed to provide subsidized office space for delegations from least-developed countries.

A number of WTO members also provide financial support for ministers and accompanying officials from least-developed countries to help them attend WTO ministerial conferences.

>>
>

The has a wide-ranging mandate. Among the broad areas of topics it has tackled as priorities are: how provisions favouring developing countries are being implemented, guidelines for technical cooperation, increased participation of developing countries in the trading system, and the position of least-developed countries.

Member-countries also have to inform the WTO about special programmes involving trade concessions for products from developing countries, and about regional arrangements among developing countries. The Trade and Development Committee handles notifications of:

Generalized System of Preferences programmes (in which developed countries lower their trade barriers preferentially for products from developing countries)

preferential arrangements among developing countries such as MERCOSUR (the Southern Common Market in Latin America), the Common Market for Eastern and Southern Africa (COMESA), and the ASEAN Free Trade Area (AFTA)

Subcommittee on Least-Developed Countries

The Subcommittee on Least-Developed Countries reports to the Trade and Development Committee, but it is an important body in its own right. Its work focuses on two related issues:

ways of integrating least-developed countries into the multilateral trading system

technical cooperation.

The subcommittee also examines periodically how special provisions favouring least-developed countries in the WTO agreements are being implemented.

The Doha agenda committees

The Doha Ministerial Conference in November 2001, added new tasks and some new working groups. The Trade and Development Committee meets in "special sessions" to handle work under the Doha Development Agenda. The ministers also set up working groups on Trade, Debt and Finance, and on Trade and Technology Transfer. (For details see the chapter on the Doha Agenda.)

The organization chart below can also be downloaded in a print-friendly pdf version:
> (87KB)
> (88KB)

Key

Reporting to General Council (or a subsidiary)

Reporting to Dispute Settlement Body

Plurilateral committees inform the General Council or

Goods Council of their activities, although these agreements are not signed by all WTO members

Trade Negotiations Committee reports to General Council

The General Council also meets as the Trade Policy Review Body and Dispute Settlement Body.

The negotiations mandated by the Doha Declaration take place in the Trade Negotiations Committee and its subsidiaries. This now includes the negotiations on agriculture and services begun in early 2000. The TNC operates under the authority of the General Council. >

Each year new chairpersons for the major WTO bodies are approved by the General Council. See the list for: > > > > > > > > > > > > > >

Any state or customs territory having full autonomy in the conduct of its trade policies may join ("accede to") the WTO, but WTO members must agree on the terms. Broadly speaking the application goes through four stages:

First, "tell us about yourself". The government applying for membership has to describe all aspects of its trade and economic policies that have a bearing on WTO agreements. This is submitted to the WTO in a memorandum which is examined by the working party dealing with the country's application. These working parties are open to all WTO members.

Second, "work out with us individually what you have to offer". When the working party has made sufficient progress on principles and policies, parallel bilateral talks begin between the prospective new member and individual countries. They are bilateral because different countries have different trading interests. These talks cover tariff rates and specific market access commitments, and other policies in goods and services. The new member's commitments are to apply equally to all WTO members under normal <u>non-discrimination rules</u>, even though they are negotiated bilaterally. In other words, the talks determine the benefits (in the form of export opportunities and guarantees) other WTO members can expect when the new member joins. (The talks can be highly complicated. It has been said that in some cases the negotiations are almost as large as an entire round of multilateral trade negotiations.)

Third, "let's draft membership terms". Once the working party has completed its examination of the applicant's trade regime, and the parallel bilateral market access negotiations are complete, the working party finalizes the terms of accession. These appear in a report, a draft membership treaty ("protocol of accession") and lists ("schedules") of the member-to-be's commitments.

Finally, "the decision". The final package, consisting of the report, protocol and lists of commitments, is presented to the WTO General Council or the Ministerial Conference. If a two-thirds majority of WTO members vote in favour, the applicant is free to sign the protocol and to accede to the organization. In many cases, the country's own parliament or legislature has to ratify the agreement before membership is complete.

>

Representing us ...

The work of the WTO is undertaken by representatives of member governments but its roots lie in the everyday activity of industry and commerce. Trade policies and negotiating positions are prepared in capitals, usually taking into account advice from private firms, business organizations, farmers, consumers and other interest groups.

Most countries have a diplomatic mission in Geneva, sometimes headed by a special ambassador to the WTO. Officials from the missions attend meetings of the many councils, committees, working parties and negotiating groups at WTO headquarters. Sometimes expert representatives are sent directly from capitals to put forward their governments' views on specific questions.

Representing groups of countries ...

Increasingly, countries are getting together to form groups and alliances in the WTO. In many cases they even speak with one voice using a single spokesman or negotiating team. In the agriculture negotiations, well over 20 coalitions have submitted proposals or negotiated with a common position, most of them still active. The increasing number of coalitions involving developing countries reflects the broader spread of bargaining power in the WTO. One group is seen as politically symbolic of this change, the G-20, which includes Argentina, Brazil, China, Egypt, India, South Africa, Thailand and many others, but there are other, overlapping "Gs" too, and one "C" — the Cotton Four (C-4), an alliance of sub-Saharan countries lobbying for trade reform in the sector.

Coalition-building is partly the natural result of economic integration — more customs unions, free trade areas and common markets are being set up around the world. It is also seen as a means for smaller countries to increase their bargaining power in negotiations with their larger trading partners and to ensure they are represented when consultations are held among smaller groups of members. Sometimes when groups of countries adopt common positions consensus can be reached more easily. Sometimes the groups are specifically created to compromise and break a deadlock rather than to stick to a common position. But there are no hard and fast rules about the impact of groupings in the WTO.

The largest and most comprehensive group is the **European Union** and its 27 member states. The EU is a customs union with a single external trade policy and tariff. While the member states coordinate their position in Brussels and Geneva, the European Commission alone speaks for the EU at almost all WTO meetings. The EU is a WTO member in its own right as are each of its member states.

A lesser degree of economic integration has so far been achieved by WTO members in the **Association of South East Asian Nations (ASEAN)** — Brunei Darussalam, Cambodia, Indonesia, Malaysia, Myanmar, Philippines, Thailand, Singapore and Viet Nam. (The remaining member Laos is applying to join the WTO.) Nevertheless, they have many common trade interests and are frequently able to coordinate positions and to speak with a single voice. The role of spokesman rotates among ASEAN members and can be shared out according to topic. **MERCOSUR, the Southern Common Market** (Argentina, Brazil, Paraguay, Uruguay and Venezuela, with Bolivia, Chile, Colombia, Ecuador and Peru as associate members), has a similar set-up.

More recent efforts at regional economic integration have not yet reached the point where their constituents frequently have a single spokesman on WTO issues. An examples is the **North American Free Trade Agreement: NAFTA** (Canada, US and Mexico). Among other groupings which occasionally present unified statements are the **African Group**, the **least-developed countries**, the **African, Caribbean and Pacific Group (ACP)** and the **Latin American Economic System (SELA)**.

A well-known alliance of a different kind is the . It was set up just before the Uruguay Round began in 1986 to argue for agricultural trade liberalization. The group became an important third force in the farm talks and remains in operation. Its members are diverse, but sharing a common objective — that agriculture has to be liberalized — and the common view that they lack the resources to compete with larger countries in domestic and export subsidies.

> Groups in the negotiations

The WTO Secretariat and budget

The WTO Secretariat is located in Geneva. It has around 630 staff and is headed by a director-general. Its responsibilities include:

Administrative and technical support for WTO delegate bodies (councils, committees, working parties, negotiating groups) for negotiations and the implementation of agreements.

Technical support for developing countries, and especially the least-developed.

Trade performance and trade policy analysis by WTO economists and statisticians.

Assistance from legal staff in the resolution of trade disputes involving the interpretation of WTO rules and precedents.

Dealing with accession negotiations for new members and providing advice to governments considering membership.

Some of the WTO's are responsible for supporting particular committees: the Agriculture Division assists the committees on agriculture and on sanitary and phytosanitary measures, for example. Other divisions provide broader support for WTO activities: technical cooperation, economic analysis, and information, for example.

The WTO budget is over 160 million Swiss francs with individual contributions calculated on the basis of shares in the total trade conducted by WTO members. Part of the WTO budget also goes to the International Trade Centre.

The Quad, the Quint, the Six and 'not'

Some of the most difficult negotiations have needed an initial breakthrough in talks among four to six "major" members.

Once upon a time, there was the "Quadrilaterals" or the "Quad":

- Canada
- European Union
- Japan
- United States

Since the turn of the century and the launch of the Doha Round, developing countries' voices have increased considerably, bringing in Brazil and India — and Australia as a representative of the Cairns Group. Japan remains in the picture not only in its own right, but also as a member of the G-10 group in agriculture. Since 2005, four, five or six of the following have got together to try to break deadlocks, particularly in agriculture.

- Australia
- Brazil
- European Union
- India
- Japan
- United States

They have been called "the new Quad", the "Four/Five Interested Parties" (FIPS), the "Quint" and the "G-6." The Doha Round was suspended in July 2006 because the six could not agree. Afterwards an alternative group of six, sometimes called the "non-G-6" or the "Oslo Group" tried their hand at compromise, sometimes listed in reverse order to emphasise their "alternative" nature — Norway, New Zealand, Kenya, Indonesia, Chile, Canada

European Union

The EU is a WTO member in its own right as are each of its 27 member states — making 28 WTO members.

While the member states coordinate their position in Brussels and Geneva, the European Commission alone speaks for the EU at almost all WTO meetings. For this reason, in most issues WTO materials refer to the EU or the more legally-correct EC.

However, sometimes references are made to the specific member states, particularly where their laws differ. This is the case in some disputes when an EU member's law or measure is cited, or in notifications of EU member countries' laws, such as in intellectual property (TRIPS). Sometimes individuals' nationalities are identified, such as for WTO committee chairpersons.

Assisting developing and transition economies

Developing countries make up about three quarters of the total WTO membership. Together with countries currently in the process of "transition" to market-based economies, they play an increasingly important role in the WTO.

Therefore, much attention is paid to the special needs and problems of developing and transition economies. The WTO Secretariat's Training and Technical Cooperation Institute organizes a number of programmes to explain how the system works and to help train government officials and negotiators. Some of the events are in Geneva, others are held in the countries concerned. A number of the programmes are organized jointly with other international organizations. Some take the form of training courses. In other cases individual assistance might be offered.

The subjects can be anything from help in dealing with negotiations to join the WTO and implementing WTO commitments to guidance in participating effectively in multilateral negotiations. Developing countries, especially the least-developed among them, are helped with trade and tariff data relating to their own export interests and to their participation in WTO bodies.

\>

Specialized help for exporting: the International Trade Centre

The International Trade Centre was established by GATT in 1964 at the request of the developing countries to help them promote their exports. It is jointly operated by the WTO and the United Nations, the latter acting through UNCTAD (the UN Conference on Trade and Development).

The centre responds to requests from developing countries for assistance in formulating and implementing export promotion programmes as well as import operations and techniques. It provides information and advice on export markets and marketing techniques. It assists in establishing export promotion and marketing services, and in training personnel required for these services. The centre's help is freely available to the least-developed countries.

The WTO in global economic policy-making

An important aspect of the WTO's mandate is to cooperate with the International Monetary Fund, the World Bank and other multilateral institutions to achieve greater coherence in global economic policy-making. A separate Ministerial Declaration was adopted at the Marrakesh Ministerial Meeting in April 1994 to underscore this objective.

The declaration envisages an increased contribution by the WTO to achieving greater coherence in global economic policy-making. It recognizes that different aspects of economic policy are linked, and it calls on the WTO to develop its cooperation with the international organizations responsible for monetary and financial matters — the World Bank and the International Monetary Fund.

The declaration also recognizes the contribution that trade liberalization makes to the growth and development of national economies. It says this is an increasingly important component in the success of the economic adjustment programmes which many WTO members are undertaking, even though it may often involve significant social costs during the transition.

Transparency (1): keeping the WTO informed

Often the only way to monitor whether commitments are being implemented fully is by requiring countries to notify the WTO promptly when they take relevant actions. Many WTO agreements say member governments have to notify the WTO Secretariat of new or modified trade measures. For example, details of any new anti-dumping or countervailing legislation, new technical standards affecting trade, changes to regulations affecting trade in services, and laws or regulations concerning the intellectual property agreement — they all have to be notified to the appropriate body of the WTO. Special groups are also established to examine new free-trade arrangements and the trade policies of countries joining as new members.

Transparency (2): keeping the public informed

The main public access to the WTO is the

website, www.wto.org. News of the latest developments are published daily. Background information and explanations of a wide range of issues — including "Understanding the WTO" — are also available. And those wanting to follow the nitty-gritty of WTO work can consult or download an ever-increasing number of official documents, now over 150,000, in Documents Online.

On 14 May 2002, the General Council decided to make more documents available to the public as soon as they are circulated. It also decided that the minority of documents that are restricted should be made public more quickly — after about two months, instead of the previous six. This was the second major decision on transparency. On 18 July 1996, the General Council had agreed to make more information about WTO activities available publicly and decided that public information, including derestricted WTO documents, would be accessible on-line.

The objective is to make more information available to the public. An important channel is through the media, with regular briefings on all major meetings for journalists in Geneva — and increasingly by email and other means for journalists around the world.

Meanwhile, over the years, the WTO Secretariat has enhanced its dialogue with civil society —

non-governmental organizations (NGOs) interested in the WTO, parliamentarians, students, academics, and other groups.

In the run-up to the Doha Ministerial Conference in 2001, WTO members proposed and agreed on several new activities involving NGOs. In 2002, the WTO Secretariat increased the number of briefings for NGOs on all major WTO meetings and began listing the briefing schedules on its website. NGOs are also regularly invited to the WTO to present their recent policy research and analysis directly to member governments.

A monthly list of NGO position papers received by the Secretariat is compiled and circulated for the information of member governments. A monthly electronic news bulletin is also available to NGOs, enabling access to publicly available WTO information

www.ingramcontent.com/pod-product-compliance
Lightning Source LLC
Chambersburg PA
CBHW051627170526
45167CB00001B/86